GCA 2007

Proceedings of the 3rd International Workshop
on Grid Computing and Applications

GCA 2007

Proceedings of the 3rd International Workshop
on Grid Computing and Applications

Biopolis, Singapore   5 – 8 June 2007

Editors

Lee Hing Yan
National Grid Office, Singapore

Lee Bu Sung
Nanyang Technological University, Singapore

Teo Yong Meng
National University of Singapore, Singapore

World Scientific

NEW JERSEY · LONDON · SINGAPORE · BEIJING · SHANGHAI · HONG KONG · TAIPEI · CHENNAI

Published by

World Scientific Publishing Co. Pte. Ltd.

5 Toh Tuck Link, Singapore 596224

USA office: 27 Warren Street, Suite 401-402, Hackensack, NJ 07601

UK office: 57 Shelton Street, Covent Garden, London WC2H 9HE

British Library Cataloguing-in-Publication Data
A catalogue record for this book is available from the British Library.

GCA 2007
Proceedings of the 3rd International Workshop on Grid Computing and Applications

Copyright © 2007 by World Scientific Publishing Co. Pte. Ltd.

ISBN-13 978-981-270-773-4
ISBN-10 981-270-773-5

Printed in Singapore.

PREFACE

Welcome to Singapore, and to the 3rd International Workshop on Grid Computing & Applications (GCA). This is the second time that GCA is held in conjunction with GridAsia. This workshop provides a forum for discussion in both the theory and applications of grid computing among researchers, developers, and user of grid computing from academia, business and industry.

A total of 14 full papers and 4 posters are selected for presentation at this workshop. Each paper is reviewed by at least two reviewers drawn from the program committee and a number of external reviewers. Accepted papers cover fundamentals of grid computing such as workflow, scheduling, resource pricing and security, and grid applications including image filtering, rendering, digital media and bioinformatics. We hope you will enjoy the program that we put together.

GCA attendees can also attend the plenary keynote addresses at GridAsia 2007. This year's keynoters include Mark Linesch (Open Grid Forum), Prof. Carol Goble (University of Manchester), and Prof. Daniel Reed (University of North Carolina, Chapel Hill).

We would like to take this opportunity to express our deepest gratitude to all who have helped make GCA 2007 a success. In particular, we thank the program committee members and referees who provided constructive and quality reviews within a very tight schedule. Special thanks go to Jon Lau for setting up the OpenConf conference management system and in facilitating the paper review process, which greatly simplified the job of the program co-chairs. This is the first time that the proceedings is published by World Scientific and we like to express our thanks to the editorial staff at World Scientific, particularly Lim Sook Cheng and Linda Kwan, for their work in the timely production of these proceedings.

Lastly, we like to convey our sincere thanks to our corporate sponsors and to A*STAR (Agency for Science, Technology and Research, Singapore) for free usage of the workshop venue.

Enjoy the workshop, and have a great time in Singapore!

Teo Yong Meng
Lee Hing Yan
Francis Lee Bu Sung

Editors

WORKSHOP COMMITTEES

General Chair: Hing-Yan LEE (National Grid Office, Singapore)

Organizing Committee

Jon LAU Khee-Erng (National Grid Office, Singapore)
Jeffrey LIM (National Grid Office, Singapore)
Vasugi d/o Velusamy (National Grid Office, Singapore)

International Program Committee

Co-Chairs: Francis LEE Bu-Sung (Nanyang Technological University, Singapore)
TEO Yong-Meng (National University of Singapore)
Members: Kento AIDA (Tokyo Institute of Technology, Japan)
Peter ARZBERGER (San Diego Supercomputing Center, USA)
Rajkumar BUYYA (University of Melbourne, Australia)
Wentong CAI (Nanyang Technological University, Singapore)
Jiannong CAO (Hong Kong Polytechnic University, Hong Kong)
Susumu DATE (Osaka University, Japan)
Sven GRAUPNER (Hewlett-Packard Labs, USA)
Seif HARIDI (Swedish Institute of Computer Science)
Terence HUNG (Institute of High Performance Computing, Singapore)
Tom JACKSON (University of York, UK)
Hai JIN (Huazhong University of Science and Technology, China)
Jysoo LEE (Korea Institute of Science and Technology Information)
Minglu LI (Shanghai Jiao Tong University, China)
LIN Fang-Pang (National Centre for High-Performance Computing, Taiwan)
Simon C. LIN (Academia Sinica Computing Centre, Taiwan)
Omer RANA (University of Cardiff, UK)
Mitsuhisa SATO (University of Tsukuba, Japan)
Simon SEE (Sun Microsystems, Singapore)
Yoshio TANAKA (National Institute of Applied Industrial Science & Technology, Japan)
Putchong UTAYOPAS (Kasetsart University, Thailand)
Vara VARAVITHYA (King Mongkut's Institute of Technology, Thailand)
Cho-Li WANG (University of Hong Kong)
Andrew WENDELBORN (University of Adelaide, Australia)

Reviewers

Christopher BAKER (Institute for Infocomm Research, Singapore)
Hing-Yan LEE (National Grid Office, Singapore)
Bertil SCHMIDT (University of NSW Asia, Singapore)
TAN Tin Wee (National University of Singapore)

CONTENTS

Grid Scheduling and Filesystem

AN ADVANCE RESERVATION-BASED COMPUTATION RESOURCE MANAGER FOR GLOBAL SCHEDULING

HIDEMOTO NAKADA, ATSUKO TAKEFUSA, KATSUHIKO OOKUBO,
TOMOHIRO KUDOH, YOSHIO TANAKA and SATOSHI SEKIGUCHI

National Institute of Advanced Industrial Science and Technology (AIST) Grid
Technology Research Center 1-18-13 Sotokanda, Chiyoda-ku, Tokyo, 1010021,
Japan,
{hide-nakada, atsuko.takefusa, ookubo-k, t.kudoh, yoshio.tanaka,
s.sekiguchi} @aist.go.jp

Advance Reservation is one possible way to enable resource co-allocation on the Grid. This method requires all the resources to have advance reservation capability as well as coordination protocol support. We employed two-phase commit protocol as a coordination protocol, which is common in the distributed transaction area, and implemented an Advance Reservation Manager called **PluS**. PluS works with existing local queuing managers, such as TORQUE or Grid Engine, and provides users advance reservation capability. To provide the capability, there are two implementation methods; 1) completely replaces the scheduling module of the queuing manger, 2) represents reservation as a queue and controls the queues using external interface. We designed and implemented a reservation manager with both way, and evaluated them. We found that the former has smaller overhead and allows arbitrary scheduling policy, while the latter is much easier to implement with acceptable response time.

1. Introduction

One of the main goals of the Grids research is to co-allocate several resources that span widely on the network, and perform huge computation on it. Advance reservation is one possible way to enable resource co-allocation on the Grid. All the resources have its own local scheduler with advance reservation capability and the super scheduler co-allocates all the resources by making reservation on all the resources on a specified timeslot.

One important thing here is the protocol between super scheduler and the local resource manager. Co-allocation of several resources is essentially a kind of distributed transaction. To guarantee acceptable behaviors on the operation failure, super scheduler and local resource managers have to employ a proper protocol between them.

Therefore, we need to have the following three things to make advance reservation based co-allocation happen: 1) A super scheduler that supports advance reservation, 2) Local schedulers that provide advance reservation, 3) Proper bridge protocols to harness 1) and 2)

We already proposed a scheduler that can co-allocate network and computation resources[6] as 1), and WSRF (Web Services Resource Framework) based advance reservation protocol[5] as 3). In this paper, we describe design and implementation of an advance reservation manager called PluS as 2). PluS supports the two-phase commit protocol, which is commonly used distributed transaction area, as a co-allocation protocol. PluS works with widely used existing local schedulers, namely, TORQUE[4] and Grid Engine[2], and provides them with advance reservation capability.

There are two methods to 'add' advance reservation capability to existing local queuing systems; 1) completely replace scheduling module in the local queuing system with the one does support the advance reservation, 2) keep the scheduling module as is and add another module that control queues to make advance reservation happen. We designed and implemented our advance reservation manager PluS in both methods and evaluated them.

The result showed that the former has smaller overhead and flexibility to allow implementers for setting up reservation policy, while it requires full re-implementation of the scheduling module putting a huge burden on the implementers. The latter is easy to implement but restricted in setting policies and have acceptable but larger overhead.

2. Coallocation and Two-Phase Commit Protocol

Here, we demonstrate the needs for commit protocol for co-allocation, showing an example. Assume that we have two resources (A and B) and already made reservation for specific timeslot on both of them, and want to move the timeslot, say, 1 hour later. In the naive implementation, it will issue modification requests to resource A and B, sequentially. However, this implementation is potentially problematic. Assume that the modification succeeded in resource A and failed in resource B. The expected behavior will be to give up the modification and revert to the original situation, keeping the original reservation time slot. Note that this is not always possible, since the reservation timeslot for resource A is already modified and there is no guarantee that the previous timeslot is still available for reservation. In the worst case, the reservation modification results in failure and the timeslot previously reserved is lost.

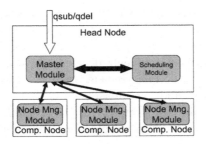

Figure 1. Generic configuration of queuing systems.

Co-allocation of several resources boils down to distributed transaction. The distributed transaction has been investigated for long time[7], and several protocols are proposed to cope with it. The most basic protocol among them is the two-phase commit protocol. The point of the protocol is to postpone the commitment of the operation until the second turn of the communication. When the super scheduler is about to perform some operation, it issues commit-requests to all the concerned local schedulers. If all the local schedulers replied ready-to-commit, the super scheduler performs commit operation. With this protocol, the situation shown above can be avoided. There are several queuing systems that support advance reservation, but none of them does support two-phase commit protocol.

3. Design of PluS

3.1. *Generic Design of Batch Queuing Systems*

In general, a batch queuing system consists of a *head node* and several *compute nodes*. The head node is the submission node through which users submit their jobs. Compute nodes are the worker nodes that actually execute jobs on requests from the head node. Note that these functions are not exclusive. It is possible for one physical node works as both of them.

The head node functionality is realized by two separate modules, typically; *master module* and *scheduling module*. The compute nodes functionality is implemented by *node management module* (figure 1).

Master module is the central module of the whole queuing system. The roll of the module can be categorized into three as follows: 1) management of job queue, 2) remote management of compute nodes, 3) initiate scheduling cycle and execution of the scheduling assignment. The master module receives job management requests, such as submission, cancellation, monitoring of jobs, from users. At also communicates with node management modules on compute nodes and keep track of the status of each node. It periodically (or on some events) initiates scheduling for the scheduling module and performs the assignments decided by the scheduling module, by giving orders to the node management modules. This module is called 'pbs_server' in TORQUE and 'sge_qmaster' in Grid Engine, respectively.

Scheduling Module is responsible for the scheduling; i.e., allocation and assignment of compute nodes to jobs. It obtains information on compute nodes and jobs and base on the information, determine the allocation and assignment. This module is called 'pbs_sched' in TORQUE and 'sge_schedd' in Grid Engine, respectively.

Node Management Module is the module that is responsible for several aspects of managing computation node, such as periodic monitoring of the load average, available memory amount, and available storage amount, and reporting them to the master module, as well as invocation, termination, monitoring of jobs. This module is called 'pbs_mom' in TORQUE, and 'sge_execd' in Grid Engine, respectively.

3.2. *Job Queue*

Job queue is a basic concept in the queuing systems. Job queue manages jobs submitted by users in (basically) FIFO (First In First Out) fashion, and schedule them one by one. Most queuing systems are capable of managing several queues. Each queue can be assigned dedicated computational nodes, enabling to manage single cluster as separated independent computing facility. Most queuing systems can be set up so that allow specific user group to submit jobs into specific queues.

3.3. *Implementation Methods for Advance Reservation*

To add the advance reservation capability to the queuing systems shown above, there are following strategies: 1) Completely replace the existing scheduling module with specially crafted module with advance reservation, 2) Control job queues and mappings with nodes and users from external module.

Scheduling Module Replace Method: In this method, scheduling module in the queuing system will be completely replaced by the newly implemented module. The module receives reservation requests from users and returns reservation IDs for each request. The users submit jobs with the reservation IDs. The master module asks the scheduling decision for the

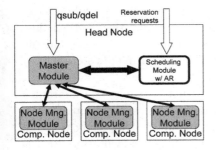
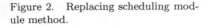
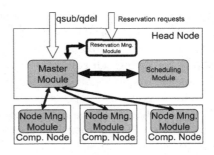

Figure 2. Replacing scheduling module method.

Figure 3. External queue control method.

replaced scheduling module, passing job information including the reservation IDs. The scheduling module will allocate node for the reserved jobs only when the timeslots are reserved for the jobs (figure 2).

This method has advantage over the other in the aspect of the policy setting latitude. This method will completely replace the 'heart' of the scheduling system, giving implementers freedom to setting arbitrary policy.

On the other hand, this method has several disadvantages especially in its implementation. Firstly, the implementers have to know the communication protocol between master module and scheduling module. Adding to it, there is no guarantee that the protocol will stay the same when the queuing system upgraded. It means that the implementers have to keep fixing the module to keep up the upgrade.

Secondly, the method requires re-implementation of the existing scheduling module functionality. Assume that we want to modify a working queuing system so that it will accept advance reservation requests. We have to re-implement all the functionality used on the site at least to guarantee the behavior of the system unchanged except for the reservations. This requires a lot of works in general.

External Queue Control Method: In this method, advance reservation capability will be implemented in the independent reservation management module, and the reserved timeslots will be represented as queues. The reservation management module will respond to the requests from users (figure 3).

The reservation management module dynamically creates queues on reservation requests from the users, and returns the name of the queue. It utilizes command line interface provided by the queuing system for creating queues. The queues will be created in *inactive* status; the queue can store jobs user submitted, but does not actually run them. It will be setup so that only the specific users can submit to it. When the reserved time arrives, the reservation management module activate the queue so that the jobs in the queue can run, as well as control the other queues so that they do not use the nodes allocated to the reservation queue.

The largest advantage of the method is that, it can easily guarantee that the behavior of the queuing system to stay the same except for the reservation. The reservation management module is completely external and do nothing without reservation request. The implementation itself is also easier. The disadvantage is that it requires queuing system to support several queue related functionalities; the queuing system have to tie a queue to specific compute node set and user set. It is not so demanding but there are several queuing systems that do not support this, including TORQUE.

The other potential disadvantage is the extra cost to control the queue using command line interface. This method requires several times queue control command invocation when processing reservation requests as well as when it makes the reservations happen.

4. Implementation of PluS

4.1. *Overview of the PluS Reservation Manager*

We implemented PluS based on two methods shown in previous section. PluS works with TORQUE and Grid Engine and it is implemented thoroughly in Java for portability and high productivity, except for few communication modules written in C for compatibility. We implemented a version for TORQUE in the scheduling module replace method and two versions for Grid Engine with both of the methods. Note that both of the two implementations with the scheduling module replace method are somewhat 'subset'; we implemented only the essential portions of the scheduling module and a few functionalities are left unimplemented. We could not implement a version for TORQUE with the queue control method, since TORQUE lacks required capability to implement the method.

PluS provides command line interface to operate with PluS. Table 1 shows a list of the command. Note that some of them have -T flag that denote 'two phase operation'. With this option the operation made by the command will not complete immediately. Instead, the operation will remain in the 'wait for commit' status. Successive `plus_commit` (or `plus_abort`) will commit (or abort) the operation. Each command is written in small shell script that wraps around a Java written client program. The program communicates with the PluS reservation management module with RMI.

Table 1. Commands for reservation management.

name	function	inputs	outputs
plus_reserve	Request Reservation	Requirements	RSV_ID
plus_cancel	Cancel Reservation	RSV_ID	
plus_modify	Modify Reservation	RSV_ID, Requirements	
plus_status	Show Reservations	RSV_ID	Reservation Status
plus_commit	Commit Reservation Operations	RSV_ID	
plus_abort	Abort Reservation Operations	RSV_ID	

The PluS reservation management module maintains the reservation table in it. The table has to be persistent to guarantee the table to survive the head node reboot or crush. We employed Java native object database *db4objects*[1]. Its interface was quite simple and easy to use and contributed to make our implementation time shorter.

4.2. *Advance Reservation Policy in PluS*

Current implementation of PluS prioritize the advance reservation over the ordinary queued jobs. The reservation is only restricted by the existence of the other reservations and is not affected by existence of the queued jobs.

I.e., jobs with advance reservation always have higher priority than the non-reserved jobs and kick out them when needed. For example, assume that a user wants to reserve a node, from 10 min. later for 1 hour. Even though all the compute nodes are occupied by non-reserved jobs and there will not be vacant nodes 10 min. later, the reservation request will succeed. 10 min. later, the PluS reservation management module kicks out a running job from a compute node so that the reserved job can use the node.

This policy is effective when the site prioritizes coordination with other resources and treats the local jobs as the backfill jobs.

4.3. *PluS for TORQUE*

TORQUE is a descendant of the OpenPBS which is an open source queuing system has been not maintained for years. Since the queues in TORQUE is not adequate for the queue control method implementation as mentioned above, we implemented the scheduling module replacement method for TORQUE.

In TORQUE the protocol used between the master module (pbs_server) and scheduling module (pbs_sched) is relatively simple, text-based protocol.

we reverse-engineered the protocol and developed a scheduling module that can communicate with this protocol.

4.4. *PluS for Grid Engine*

Grid Engine is a queuing scheduler developed by Sun Microsystems, which is widely used for many projects in the world. We implemented PluS with both of the two methods. The scheduling module replacement method for Grid Engine is done in just the same way with TORQUE, except for the fact that the protocol used there is a binary and we have to implement a module to translate plain XML notation. Implementation with the queue control method works as shown in figure 4.

5. Evaluation

In this section we show comparisons between the scheduling module replacement method and the queue control method. We evaluate ease of implementation based on number of lines of code and command execution speed for reserve/cancel operation.

5.1. *Evaluation Based on Lines of Codes*

Here, we show the lines of codes required for each implementations. Currently, we have three PluS implementations; for TORQUE, for SGE with replacement method, and for SGE with queue control method. We counted the number of lines of codes for each implementation. While the number of lines might not accurately reflect easiness of implementation, especially the implementation languages span from C to Java and sh, it still makes fair index for easiness. The three implementations share some portions of codes, such as for reservation and allocation management, command line interface, as well as dedicated codes specific for each implementation. Figure 5 shows the number of lines for each implementation. The shared 8000 lines are shown as the underlying portion.

The dedicated portion is about 3000 lines for TORQUE, about 5200 lines for scheduling module replacement version for Grid Engine, and about 1800 lines for queue control version for Grid Engine. We can see that queue control version requires smallest dedicated code, proving that easiness of implementation of the method. Please note that the two implementations for scheduling module replacement method are not complete, i.e., they do not support whole functionality the original scheduling module has. It

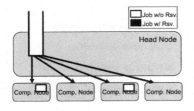

(A) Initial Status. The queue shown left is the default queue that is tied up to all the compute nodes.

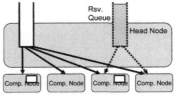

(B) Reservation made. When the reservation management module receives a reservation request from user, it creates a queue (on the right) in suspended status and returns the name of the queue as the reservation ID. The queue is tied to specific compute nodes, but is not allowed to assign jobs to the nodes.

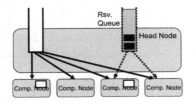

(C) The users submit jobs to the newly created queue. The jobs will not be assigned until the reservation start time, since the queue is created as suspended.

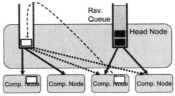

(D) Reservation period starts. The queue is activated. If the compute nodes already have running jobs, PluS kills the jobs and resubmits them to the original queue, with *qresub* command. The jobs will start over on the other compute nodes. The default queue has lost control over the two queues on the right.

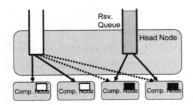

(E) During the reservation period. The preempted job is re-assigned to the other compute node.

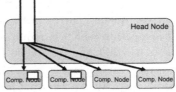

(F) Reservation period is over. The reservation management module deactivates and removes the reservation queue. If some jobs for the queue are still running, reservation management module will kill them. It also reconfigure other queues so that they can use the compute nodes

Figure 4. Implementation with the queue control method.

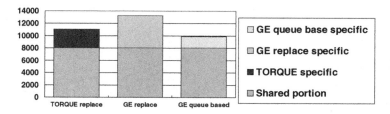

Figure 5.   Evaluation based on number of lines.

means that implementation of the whole functionality will require much more lines of codes.

5.2. Time to Make/Cancel Reservations

There is anticipation on the queue control method; it might have extra overhead on reservation operations due to queue control commands issue. We evaluated the overhead by comparing the execution time with PluS implementation for Grid Engine with both methods.

The evaluation was performed on a small cluster with one head node and four compute nodes with Pentium III 1.4 GHz Dual CPUs, with 2 GBytes memory, Redhat 8 Linux installed. We measured time spent for making and canceling reservation using the *time* command.

We performed 10 experiments for each and got average number; 1.02[s] for reservation and 0.92[s] for cancellation with the Scheduling Module Replacement Method, and 1.95[s] for reservation and 1.02[s] for cancellation with the Queue Control Method. We can see that while both of them are acceptably fast with the scheduling module replacement method is slightly faster than the queue control method. The difference comes from *qconf* command invocation which is required only in the queue control method. We can also see that the difference between two methods is substantial for making reservation, while it is not for cancellation. This is because four *qconf* invocations are required for making reservation, while just one is required for cancellation.

6. Related Work

Several commercial batch queuing systems, such as PBS Professional or LSF, have advance reservation capability. There are also plug-in scheduling modules for existing batch queuing system, that support advance reservation, such as Maui and Catalina, They all does not provide two-phase commit protocol. The reason why they do not support two-phase commit is that they are not meant for fully automatic co-allocation but for reservation only for the single site.

Maui Scheduler[3] is a plug-in scheduler for TORQUE,[a] which is developed by the Cluster Resources Inc., the maintainer of the TORQUE. Maui scheduler is implemented in the scheduling module replacement method, i.e., it completely replaces the scheduling module of TORQUE.

Catalina[8] is a scheduling module that can work with TORQUE and Load Leveler. It is used in the Tera Grid project in US. Catalina provides advance reservation capability, which is called 'User-Settable Reservation', in Catalina terminology. Catalina is implemented in the scheduling module replacement method. Another significant feature of Catalina is that it is totally written in Python, allowing administrators to modify parameters embedded in the source code.

Catalina prioritize jobs from ordinary queues over the reservation, while PluS prioritize the reservation. Reservations are possible only when there are no jobs scheduled for the time period, from the ordinary queue.

7. Conclusion

We proposed a reservation management system PluS that supports two-phase commit protocol, to allow safe and efficient resource co-allocation on the Grids. PluS works with existing queuing system such as TORQUE or Grid Engine and provides them with advance reservation capability. We proposed two implementation methods; scheduling module replacement method and queue control method, and actually implemented PluS in both way, and evaluated them.

We found that both of them have advantage and disadvantage. The former has smaller overhead and flexibility to allow implementers for setting up reservation policy, while it requires full re-implementation of the scheduling module putting a huge burden on the implementers. The latter is easy to implement but restricted in setting policy and have acceptable but larger overhead.

For future work, we will address the following issues.

Resource specification improvements: Current implementation assumes that the compute nodes are homogeneous and does not allow specifying the resource characteristics, such as architecture, amount of memory or disk space size. We will address this.

---

[a]Maui did work with Grid Engine previously, but current version does not.

Sophisticated reservation policy: As described in 4.2, current implementation always gives highest priority on the reservation and the reservations are made first-comes-first-served base. Obviously, these will not be acceptable for the production cluster administrators. We are designing a mechanism to allow administrators to setup there own policy in a simple script language, so that each administrator can describe a policy suitable for his/her system.

Application to the other queuing systems: The queue control method implementation will be easily applicable to the other queuing systems, if the system supports queue control mechanism required by PluS. We will confirm the easiness through application of the method to the other queuing systems, such as Load Leveler or Condor.

Acknowledgement

This work is partly funded by the Science and Technology Promotion Program's "Optical Paths Network Provisioning based on Grid Technologies" of MEXT, Japan.

References

1. db4objects. http://www.db4o.com/.
2. Grid Engine. http://gridengine.sunsource.net.
3. Maui cluster scheduler. http://www.clusterresources.com/pages/products/-maui-cluster-scheduler.php.
4. TORQUE Resource Manager. http://www.clusterresources.com/pages/products/torque-resource-manager.php.
5. Hidemoto Nakada, Atsuko Takefusa, Katsuhiko Ookubo, Makoto Kishimoto, Tomohiro Kudoh, Yoshio Tanaka, and Satoshi Sekiguchi. Design and implementation of a local scheduling system with advance reservation for co-allocation on the grid. In *Proceedings of CIT2006*, 2006.
6. Atsuko Takefusa, Michiaki Hayashi, Naohide Nagatsu, Hidemoto Nakada, Tomohiro Kudoh, Takahiro Miyamoto, Tomohiro Otani, Hideaki Tanaka, Masatoshi Suzuki, Yasunori Sameshima, Wataru Imajuku, Masahiko Jinno, Yoshihiro Takigawa, Shuichi Okamoto, Yoshio Tanaka, and Satoshi Sekiguchi. G-lambda: Coordination of a grid scheduler and lambda path service over gmpls. *Future Generation Computing Systems*, 22(2006):868–875, 2006.
7. Andrew S. Tannenbaum. *Distributed Operating Systems*. Prentice Hall, 1994.
8. Kenneth Yoshimoto, Patricia Kovatch, and Phil Andrews. Co-scheduling with user-settable reservations. In Dror G. Feitelson, Eitan Frachtenberg, Larry Rudolph, and Uwe Schwiegelshohn, editors, *Job Scheduling Strategies for Parallel Processing*, pages 146–156. Springer Verlag, 2005.

REPUTATION BASED JOB SCHEDULING IN DESKTOP GRIDS

XIAOHU LIU, CONGFENG JIANG and CHENG WANG

Engineering Computing and Simulation Institute, Huazhong University of Science and Technology, Wuhan 430074, China

YINGHUI ZHAO

Digital Engineering and Simulation Center, Huazhong University of Science and Technology, Wuhan 430074, China

Desktop Grid is usually used to execute a lot of user jobs at dispersed sites. However, how to trust a grid site and where to schedule the user jobs is a key factor that affects success rate, security, and fault tolerance of the job scheduling. A computational model of reputation in desktop grid is proposed and the user jobs are always scheduled to sites with *just high* reputation values. In order to avoid reputation-competing problem (i.e., all jobs scheduled to the site with the highest reputation values), we introduce the *reputation values balancing* concept similar to load balancing. A reputation balancing algorithm is proposed which aims to minimize the deviation of reputation values and the number of jobs scheduled to a grid site is proportional to the site's reputation value. Simulation results on RSBSME (Remote Sensing Based Soil Moisture Extraction) workload in a real desktop grid environment show that the performance of the proposed reputation model is effective, fault tolerant and scalable.

1. Introduction

A desktop grid [1, 2] consists of large set of Internet or local area network connected heterogeneous PCs with various operating systems, hardware architectures, and resource management mechanisms. In the past few years, desktop grid has emerged as an important methodology to utilize idle resources of desktop PCs. Desktop grids such as the SETI@Home Project [3] have shown global popularity and harness the aggregate computing power to tens of TFlops. For example, in [1], the 28-day measurement results showed that the desktop grid consisting of 220 hosts at the San Diego Supercomputer Center (SDSC) (with CPU clock rates ranging from 179MHz up to 3.0GHz, with an average of 1.19GHz) is equivalent to a 209-node cluster on weekends, and to a 160-node cluster on weekdays, for 56 million operation tasks (approximately 25 minutes on a 1.5 GHz CPU).

Desktop grids are mostly oriented toward high throughput computing for processing a large number of independent tasks in scientific or business applications. Usually, the desktop grids take a long period of time, maximizing the number of tasks processed per time unit. A lot of algorithms have been developed for scheduling jobs in desktop grids [4, 5, 6, and 7]. Unfortunately, most of the existing proposed scheduling algorithms had ignored the security problem while scheduling jobs onto geographically distributed grid sites with a handful of exceptions. In a real desktop grid, security threats always exist and the jobs are subject to failures or delays caused by local interruption, network connection delays or timeouts, hardware or software vulnerability, and system crashes. Consequently, the assumption that the grid environments are safe and the resources are 100% reliable is no longer applicable for job scheduling in real desktop grids. Thus the existing proposed heuristics are not applicable in a risky desktop grid environment without modifications.

Volunteer resources volatility is the main character and a major challenge of desktop grid when scheduling jobs in a risky or unsafe desktop grid environment [4, 8], especially in an Internet-based desktop grid environment. In a real desktop grid, computers are usually assigned to a person who not only uses the machine but also fully controls the resource. And each site may have different usage modes, security policies, trust model or reputation system model. Thus, among the large number of issues raised by desktop grids (security, privacy, coordination, scheduling, load balancing, etc.) [2], how to trust a grid site and where to schedule the user jobs is a key factor that affects success rate, security, and fault tolerance of the job scheduling. Reputation system is widely used for desktop grid to evaluate the reputation of a grid site, i.e., the trust degree of a grid site. However, very few investigate the issue of reputation competing problem (i.e., all jobs scheduled to the site with the highest reputation values). In this paper we investigate *reputation balancing* (like the concept of load balancing) in a wider perspective, and a reputation balancing algorithm is proposed which aims to minimize the deviation of reputation values. Simulation results in a real desktop grid environment show that the performance of the proposed model is fault-tolerant and scalable.

The rest of the paper is organized as follows: Section 2 presents a brief review of related work. In Section 3, we present a computational model of reputation values and specify the job scheduling strategy based on it. We present extensive simulation results on RSBSME (Remote Sensing Based Soil Moisture Extraction) workload in a real desktop grid environment in Section 4. Finally, we summarize the contributions and make some remarks on further research in Section 5.

2. Related Works

In a desktop grid, machines join and exit the grid systems frequently at any period of time without prior notification. Events such as system shutdown or crash, communication timeout due to long network stall or high congestion, and management policy restricting node and network utilization for grid applications only on idle time, could result in job failures [2]. Thus, the sites that finish previous jobs fast and successfully should be placed more jobs in the next round of job scheduling than those sites that with high job failures. Using some performance monitoring tools, for example, DGMonitor [9], the performance or behavior of a site can be traced and recorded. The reputation representing the availability probability of a site can be obtained based on the collected performance data.

Gupta *et al* [10] proposed a reputation and incentive system for unstructured Peer-to-Peer networks and the reputation values are computed using debit-credit reputation computation (DCRC) and credit-only reputation computation (CORC). In their work, the peer reputations are periodically updated in a secure, light-weight, and partially distributed manner.

Song *et al* [11, 12] developed a security-binding scheme through site reputation assessment and trust integration across grid sites. They applied fuzzy theory to handle the fuzziness or uncertainties behind all trust attributes. The binding is achieved by periodic exchange of site security information and matchmaking to satisfy user job demands. In this paper, we try to quantify the reputation of resource sites, based on previous performance data, such as prior successful job execution rates, cumulative site utilization, and bandwidth between grid sites.

Choi [4] categorize failures of volunteer resources in two main classes: volatility failures and interference failures. Hwang [13] presented a generic failure detection mechanism and a flexible failure handling framework as a fault-tolerant mechanism on the grid. They use notification mechanism to transfer failure messages between grid sites. In this paper, our work is partially based on the above notification mechanism. We assume that there is a centric scheduler to transfer failure messages between grid sites when jobs failed or successfully completed.

3. Computational Model of Reputation

Our work is based on the related works on reputation system, grid security, trust management, and fault-tolerant job scheduling. Our approach schedules user jobs to grid sites with high reputation values, which extends reputation-based grid job scheduling in the direction of reputation balancing. We try to seek a balancing point between the speed performance and trust assurance such as successful scheduling rates. Security threats, system failures, and doubtful trustworthiness of remote sites have created barriers in trusted job scheduling to remote desktop grid sites, especially in an internet-connected desktop grid environment. In our work, the computational model assesses the resource site's reputations, namely, the Reputation Values (RV).RV quantifies how much a user can trust a site for successfully executing a given job. Only the job can be successfully finished when RV is high enough when scheduling the jobs.

3.1. *Assumptions*

In this paper, we define resource as any capability that can be scheduled, assigned, or controlled by the underlying implementation to assure non-conflicting usage by processes as in [14]. Example of resources includes processors and storage devices. A host, machine, or site refers to a PC in a desktop grid and the terms are used interchangeably. And the terms jobs, tasks, and applications are used interchangeably to refer to a request made by a user to run a given application with some given input. The following assumptions are made in this paper:

(1) The applications have been divided into sub tasks and each sub task is independent;
(2) The tasks have no priorities;
(3) The estimates of expected task execution times on each machine in the desktop grid sites are known. This assumption is commonly made when studying scheduling problems for grids or heterogeneous computing systems (e.g., [15, 16, 17]). Approaches such as code profiling, analytic benchmarking, and statistical prediction for doing this estimation can be found in [18, 19].
(4) The system components may fail and can be eventually recovered from failures.
(5) Job failures can occur online at any time and the site failures are independent from each other.
(6) When the primary scheduler fails, there are backup schedulers to take over all the work of the primary scheduler.
(7) There is a job table maintained by a centric server and all the information of running or finished jobs can be queried through the job table.

3.2. *Computational Model of Reputation*

Let M denote a hosts set, $M = \{m_j \mid j = 1, 2, 3, ..., m\}$. Let T denote tasks set, $T = \{t_i \mid i = 1, 2, 3, ..., n\}$. We define the following parameters:

(1) RV_j : The reputation value of host m_j. RV_j is in the range [0, 1] with 0 for the most risky resource site and 1 for a risk-free or fully trusted site.

(2) $\overline{RV}$: The average reputation value of the whole desktop grid environment, i.e., the global reputation value. $\overline{RV}$ is in the range [0, 1] with 0 for the most risky desktop grid environment and 1 for a risk-free or fully trusted desktop grid environment. In other words, $\overline{RV}$ stands for the trust degree of the desktop grid environment.

(3) p_j : The speed of host m_j (MFlops).

We determine the reputation values of a grid site using four variables: the time interval from the last successful task execution, the accumulative successful execution rate, the accumulative utilization rate, and network bandwidth. In a full-scale desktop grid reputation system, the number of variables related to reputation values could be extended to several hundreds. However, we list four frequently used variables we applied in our experiments. The computational model of the reputation value of host m_j is shown as following:

$$RV_j = \alpha \times e^{-TI_j} + \beta \times rs_j + \gamma \times ru_j + \eta \times bw_j \tag{1}$$

Where:

TI_j : denotes the time interval from the last successful task execution on host m_j, $TI_j > 0$;

rs_j : denotes the accumulative successful job execution rate of host m_j, $0 < rs_j < 1$;

ru_j : denotes the accumulative utilization rate of host m_j, $0 < ru_j < 1$;

bw_j : denotes the bandwidth between host m_j and other grid sites;

α, β, γ, η: weighted factors of time interval from the last successful task execution, accumulative successful job execution rate, accumulative utilization rate, and bandwidth, respectively. They are in the same range (0, 1) with $\alpha + \beta + \gamma + \eta = 1$;

$\overline{RV}$ is computed as following:

$$\overline{RV} = \frac{\sum_{j=1}^{m} RV_j \times p_j}{\sum_{j=1}^{m} p_j} + \frac{\sum_{j=1}^{m} RV_j \times bw_j}{\sum_{j=1}^{m} bw_j} \tag{2}$$

In order to evaluate the global reputation value of the desktop grid environment, let σ_{host} denote the deviation of the desktop grid environment, i.e.

$$\sigma_{host} = \frac{\sum_{j=1}^{m} (RV_j - \overline{RV})^2}{m} \tag{3}$$

The amount of variance among the reputation values of hosts in the desktop grid environment is defined as *reputation heterogeneity*. High global *reputation heterogeneity* was represented by $\sigma_{host} \geq 0.6$ and low *reputation heterogeneity* by $\sigma_{host} \leq 0.1$. These heterogeneity ranges are based on the expected desktop grid environments. The ranges are chosen to reflect the fact that in real situations there is more variability across reputation values for different hosts and different desktop grid environments.

In this paper, we regard the reputation of a host as one kind of computing power and the reputation is one capability that could be consumed by user jobs. In a real load balancing scenario, we try to balance the load distribution among multiple grid sites. The same concept can be borrowed here. If a host with the highest reputation value is occupied by many user jobs while all other hosts with relative smaller reputation value are idle, we call this a *reputation load unbalancing*. Similarly, in a greedy scheduling situation, all user jobs will be scheduled to the fastest host in the grid environment. We use a mixture strategy of load balancing and reputation balancing when scheduling jobs. For example, the number of jobs scheduled to a grid site is proportional to its reputation values. Let k_j denote the number of jobs scheduled to host m_j, then k_j can be calculated as following:

$$k_j = \frac{RV_j}{\sum_{j=1}^{m} RV_j} \times n \tag{4}$$

In our experiments, we round k_j to the nearest upper integer. For example, if the computed k_j is 0.3, then the rounded k_j is 1.

3.3. Scheduling Algorithm

Figure 1 is the pseudo-code of the job scheduling algorithm using the proposed reputation assessment and *reputation balancing* strategy. When the number of jobs in the job set becomes a fixed maximum number, like 100, we call this a scheduling event. When scheduling event occurs, the scheduler first computes RV_j, $\overline{RV}$, and k_j. Then, the scheduler schedule tasks to host m_j. At the same time, the status of entire running jobs is recorded and stored in the job table. If the scheduler receives a job completion message from one of the remote host, it will record the job information in the job table and update its accumulative successful execution rate. If a job failure is detected, an alternative site in the desktop grid will be selected.

Job Scheduling Algorithm

1. compute RV_j, $\overline{RV}$, and k_j
2. sort hosts by reputation values in descending order
3. for each host in M
4.   schedule k_j tasks to host m_j
5.   delete the task from T
6.   update job table
7. end for
8. repeat{
9. for each task in T
10. if any job is done successfully
11.   update job table and the corresponding accumulative successful execution rate
12. else if any job failed
13.   reschedule the job to an alternative site randomly
14.   update job table
15. end if
16. end for
17. }

Figure 1. Job scheduling algorithm based on reputation assessment and reputation balancing.

4. Simulation Results

We test the performance of the proposed reputation assessment and reputation balancing model on RSBSME (Remote Sensing Based Soil Moisture Extraction) workload. The RSBSME workload is a typical data intensive, compute intensive and high throughput computing application. The RSBSME is defined as a set of independent parallel jobs and each job compute a part of a large remote sensing image containing soil moisture information. Here, we use an approximate 165,000 square kilometers remote sensing image of Hubei Province of China. To model the heterogeneity of the desktop grid sites, each site has different initial reputation value.

Table 1 lists the key simulation parameters. The simulation results are shown in Table 2. Due to space limitations, we present a subset of the performance results in Table 2. All the data in Table 2 are mean values of 10 simulation results. In our simulations, we observed that the performance of the grid is best when α, β, γ, η are set to 0.15, 0.4, 0.25, 0.20, respectively. Thus, the results in Table 2 are obtained when α, β, γ, η are set to 0.15, 0.4, 0.25, 0.20, respectively. In our simulation, a job will be dropped if it has been rescheduled for more than ten times.

Table 1. Simulation Parameters and Settings.

Items	Values
Number of jobs	10,000
Number of sites	8
Site processing speed	300MFlops
Initial reputation values	Normally distributed in [0, 1]
Sites failure rate	Poisson distribution with failure rate 0.10
Expected execution times	normally distributed in [120, 400] sec
bandwidth between sites	100 Mbps

The results in Table 2 suggest that the makespan and job scheduling success rate of the proposed reputation model is relatively good and the scheduling scales well when the number of tasks is large. The job scheduling success rate is high enough due to the rescheduling mechanism when job failed in a real desktop grid environment. Moreover, the grid utilization and tasks average waiting time are acceptable in a real desktop grid environment

Table 2. Simulation Results.

Metrics	Values
Tasks makespan	32,120,000sec
Job scheduling success rate	87.3%
Grid utilization	51.5%
Tasks average waiting time	1,237sec

In summary, in our model, the number of jobs scheduled to a given site is proportional to its reputation values, which avoids the reputation-competing problem or *reputation load unbalancing*. In a real dynamic, cross-domains, local area network connected or internet connected desktop grid, our reputation model is applicable with high job scheduling success rate, moderate grid utilization, and scalability.

5. Conclusions and Future Work

In this paper, we proposed a computational model of reputation in desktop grid. In this model, the user jobs are scheduled to sites with *just high* reputation values. In order to avoid *reputation load unbalancing*, the number of jobs scheduled to a given site is proportional to its reputation values, which is similar to load balancing. Simulation results in a real desktop grid environment show that the performance of the proposed model is relatively good for job execution.

In our future work, we will construct a fault tolerance model based on our reputation computing model and a fault-detection mechanism allowing for failed job rescheduling will be included. And we will plan to simulate the proposed algorithm using extensive workload characteristics.

Acknowledgments

The funding support of this work by Innovation Fund of Huazhong University of Science and Technology under contract No.HF04012006271 is appreciated.

References

1. D. Kondo, M. Taufer, I. Brooks, L. Charles, H. Casanova and A. Chien, Proceedings of 18th International Parallel and Distributed Processing Symposium, 353(2004).
2. S. Djilali, T. Herault, O. Lodygensky, T. Morlier, G. Fedak and F. Cappello, Proceedings of IEEE/ACM SC2004 Conference, 13(2004).
3. SETI@home Project, http://setiathome.ssl.berkeley.edu.
4. S. Choi, M. Baik, C. Hwang, J. Gil and H. Yu, Proceedings of 3rd IEEE International Symposium on Network Computing and Applications (NCA'04), 366(2004).
5. D. Kondo, A. Chien and H. Casanova, Proceedings of IEEE/ACM SC2004 Conference, 499(2004).
6. P. Domingues, P. Marques and L. Silva, Proceedings of the 14th Euromicro International Conference on Parallel, Distributed, and Network Based Processing, 83(2006).

7. S. Choi, M. Baik, J. Gil, C. Park, S. Jung and C. Hwang, Proceedings of 4th International Conference on Grid and Cooperative Computing, LNCS3795, 811(2005).

8. J. Brevik, D. Nurmi and R. Wolski, Proceedings of 2004 IEEE International Symposium on Cluster Computing and the Grid, 190(2004).

9. P. Cicotti, M. Taufer, A. Chien, Proceedings of 18th International Parallel and Distributed Processing Symposium, 3373(2004).

10. M. Gupta, P. Judge and M. Ammar, Proceedings of 13th International Workshop on Network and Operating Systems Support for Digital Audio and Video, 144(2003).

11. S. Song and K. Hwang, Proceedings of the ISCA 17th International Conference on Parallel and Distributed Computing Systems, 110(2004).

12. S. Song, K. Hwang, R. Zhou and Y. Kwok, IEEE Internet Computing, **9(6)**, 24(2005).

13. S. Hwang, PhD thesis, University of Southern California, 2003.

14. J.H. Abawajy, Proceedings of IEEE 18th International Parallel and Distributed Processing Symposium, 238(2004).

15. T.D. Braun, D. Hensgen, R. Freund R *et al*, Journal of Parallel and Distributed Computing, **61(6)**, 810(2001).

16. J. Kim, S. Shivle, H.J. Siegel *et al*, Journal of Parallel and Distributed Computing, **67(2)**, 154(2007).

17. H. Zhao H. and R. Sakellariou, Proceedings of 20th International Parallel and Distributed Processing Symposium, 1(2006).

18. S. Ali, H.J. Siegel, M. Maheswaran *et al*, Proceedings of 9th Heterogeneous Computing Workshop, 185(2000).

19. M.A. Iverson, F. Özgüner and L. Potter, IEEE Transactions on Computers, **48(12)**, 1374(1999).

A DATAFLOW MODEL FOR .NET-BASED GRID COMPUTING SYSTEMS

CHAO JIN and RAJKUMAR BUYYA

Grid Computing and Distributed Systems Laboratory
Department of Computer Science and Software Engineering
the University of Melbourne, Melbourne, VIC, Australia

LEX STEIN and ZHENG ZHANG

System Research Group
Microsoft Research Asia, Beijing, China

This paper presents the design, implementation and evaluation of a dataflow system, including a dataflow programming model and a dataflow engine, for coarse-grained distributed data intensive applications. The dataflow programming model provides users with a transparent interface for application programming and execution management in a parallel and distributed computing environment. The dataflow engine dispatches the tasks onto candidate distributed computing resources in the system, and manages failures and load balancing problems in a transparent manner. The system has been implemented over .NET platform and deployed in a Windows Desktop Grid. This paper uses two benchmarks to demonstrate the scalability and fault tolerance properties of our system.

1. Introduction

Due to the growing popularity of networked computing environments and the emergence of multi-core processors, parallel and distributed computing is now required at all levels of application development, from desktops to Internet-scale computing environments, such as Grid [6] and P2P. However, programming on distributed resources, especially for parallel applications, is more difficult than programming on centralized environment. There are many research systems that simplify distributed computing. These include BOINC [3], XtremWeb [5], Alchemi [1], and JNGI [9]. These systems divide a job into a number of independent tasks. Applications that can be parallelized in this way are called "embarrassingly parallel". However many algorithms can not be expressed as independent tasks because of internal data dependencies.

The work presented in this paper aims towards supporting advanced applications containing multiple tasks with data dependency relationships. Many resource-intensive applications consist of multiple modules, each of which receives input data, performs computations and generates output. Scientific applications for this nature include genomics [16], simulation [8], data mining [12] and graph computing [18]. In many cases for these applications, a module's output becomes an input other modules. A coarse grained dataflow model [19] can be used to describe such applications.

We use a dataflow programming model to compose a dataflow graph for specifying the data dependency relationship within a distributed application. Under the dataflow interface, we use a dataflow engine to explore the graph to schedule tasks across distributed resources and automatically handle the cumbersome problems, such as scalable performance, fault tolerance, load balancing, etc. Within this process, users do not need to worry about the details of processes, threads and explicit communication.

The main contributions of this work are: 1) A simple and powerful dataflow programming model, which supports the composition of parallel applications for deployment in a distributed environment; 2) An architecture and runtime machinery that supports scheduling of the dataflow computation in dynamic environments, and handles failures transparently; 3) A detailed analysis of dataflow model using two sample applications over a Desktop Grid.

The remainder of this paper is organized as follows. Section 2 provides a discussion on related work. Section 3 describes the dataflow programming model with examples. Section 4 presents the architecture and design for a dataflow system over .NET platform. Section 5 presents experimental evaluation results. Section 6 concludes the paper with pointer to future work.

2. Related Work

Dataflow concept was first presented by Dennis et al. [19]. Since then several researchers have investigated various aspects of dataflow models for parallel and distributed systems and applications. As the pure dataflow is fine-grained, its practical implementation has been found to be an arduous task. Thus optimized versions of dataflow models have also been presented, including dynamic dataflow model and synchronous dataflow model [10]. Its usage continued to investigate for coarse-grained parallel applications.

River [13] provides a dataflow programming environment for scientific database like applications on clusters through a visual interface. River focuses on solving transient heterogeneity problems rather than fault tolerance problem in dynamic environment.

Grid systems such as Condor [4], Gridbus Workflow Engine [21], and Pegasus [20] provide mechanisms for workflow scheduling. Workflow systems are trying to seek opportunities for concurrency at the level of tasks. However, how to easily achieve the concurrency within each task has been ignored. Kepler [15] provides a graph based interface for scientific workflow scheduling, and Grid superscalar [14] allows users to write their applications in a sequential way. However they do not focus on handling failures.

MapReduce [7] is a cluster middleware designed to help programmers to transform and aggregate key-value pairs by automating parallelism and failure recovery. Their programming model can also be taken as a fixed static dataflow graph.

3. Programming Model

Dataflow programming model abstracts the process of computation as a *dataflow graph* consisting of *vertices* and directed *edges*.

The *vertex* embodies two entities:

a) The data created during the computation or the initial input data;
b) The execution module to generate the corresponding vertex data.

The directed *edge* connects vertices, which indicates the dependency relationship between vertices. A vertex, takes its dependent vertices as its inputs.

A vertex is an *initial vertex* if there are no edges pointing to it but it has edges pointing to other vertices; correspondingly, a vertex is called a *result vertex* if it has no edges pointing to other vertices and there are some edges pointing to it. An initial vertex does not have an associated execution module.

Our current programming model focuses on supporting a static dataflow graph for SPMD (Single Program Multiple Data) applications, which means the number of vertices and their relationships are known before execution. We expect the graph to be a Directed Acyclic Graph (DAG).

3.1. Namespace for Vertices

Each vertex has a unique name in the dataflow graph. The name consists of 3 parts: *Category*, *Version* and *Space*. Thus, the name is denoted as *<C, T, S>*. *Category* denotes different kinds of vertices; *Version* denotes the index for the vertex along the time axis during the computing process; *Space* denotes the vertex's index along the space axis during execution. In the following text, we call vertex name as *name*.

3.2. Dataflow Library API

3.2.1. Specifying Execution Module

To specify instructions/code to be executed, which is called execution module and used to generate the output for each vertex, users need to inherit the *Module* class in dataflow library for writing each vertex's execution code. In particular, users need to implement 3 virtual functions:

- *ModuleName* **SetName**() : specify a name for the execution module, which is used as an identifier during editing the data dependency graph.
- void **Compute**(*Vertex*[] *inputs*) : implemented by users for generating output taking input vertex data. The input data is denoted by *inputs*. Each element of *inputs* consists of a *name* and a data buffer.
- byte[] **SetResult**():called by the system to get the output data after Compute() is finished.

3.2.2. Composing Dataflow Graph

The *dataflow* API provides two functions for composing the static data dependency graph:

- **CreateVertex**(*vertex*, *ModuleName*) : is used to specify the name and corresponding execution module for each vertex.
- **Dependency**(*vertex*, *InputVertex*): is used to add *y* as *x*'s dependent vertex.

Two functions are provided to set the initial and result vertices as follows:

- **SetInitialVertex**(vertex, file)
- **SetResultVertex**(vertex, file)

3.3. Example

Given the matrix vector iterative multiplication, $V^t = M * V^{t-1}$. We partition the matrix and vector by rows into *m* pieces respectively, as $V_i^t = \sum_{j=1}^{m} M_i * V_j^{t-1} (i = 1...m)$.

The corresponding dataflow graph is illustrated by **Figure 1**. To name vertices, *Category = M* denotes the matrix vertices and *Category = V* denotes the vector vertices. For *i*-th vector vertex, the data relationship should be specified as: $<V, t, i> \leftarrow \{<M, 0, i>, <V, t-1, j>\}$ (j=1...m).

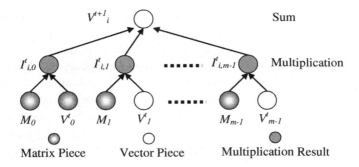

Figure 1: Dataflow graph for the i-th vector piece.

4. Architecture and Design

This section describes a dataflow architecture designed for a Windows Desktop Grid consisting of commodity PCs based on .NET platform. The environment consists of idle desktops that are used for computing but drop out of the system as soon as interactive programs are started by the users on them. Such nodes can rejoin the system when they are idle again.

4.1. *System Overview*

The dataflow system consists of a single master and multiple workers as illustrated in **Figure 2**. The master is responsible for accepting jobs from users, organizing multiple workers to work cooperatively, sending executing requests to workers and handling failures of workers. Each worker contributes CPU and disk resources to the system and waits for executing requests from the master.

4.2. *The Structure of the Master*

The master is responsible for monitoring the status of each worker, dispatching ready tasks to suitable workers and tracking the progress of each job according to the data dependency graph. On the master, there are 4 key components:

- *Membership component*: maintains the list of available worker nodes. When some nodes join or leave the system, the list is updated correspondingly. The membership is maintained through heartbeat signal between master and workers. The heartbeat signal also carries the status information about the worker, such as CPU, memory and disk usage.

- *Registry component*: maintains the location information for available vertex data. In particular, it maintains a list of indices for each available vertex data. Each vertex has an index, which lists workers that hold its data.
- *Dataflow Graph component*: maintains the data dependency graph for each job, keeps track of the availability of vertices and explores ready tasks. When it finds ready tasks, it will notify the scheduler component.
- *Scheduler component*: dispatches ready tasks to suitable workers for executing. For each task, the master notifies workers of inputs & initiates the associated execution module to generate the output data.

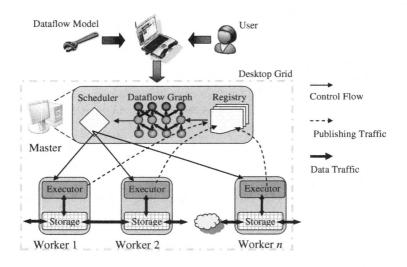

Figure 2: Architecture of dataflow-based desktop Grid computing system.

4.3. *The Structure of a Worker*

Workers work in a peer to peer fashion. To cooperate with the master, each worker has two functions: executing upon requests from master and storing the vertex data. Correspondingly there are 2 important components on each worker:

- *Executor component*: receives executing requests from the master, fetches input from the storage component, generates output to the storage component and notifies *master* about the available vertex of the output data.

- *Storage component*: is responsible for managing and holding vertex data generated by executors and providing it upon requests. Actually the storage components across workers run as a distributed storage service. To handles failures, upon request from master, the storage component can keep data persistently locally or replicate some vertices on remote side to improve the reliability and availability.

4.4. *System Interaction*

Upon receiving submission from users, including the dataflow graph and execution modules, the master node will create an instance as a thread for each module. Based on .NET platform, the master serializes the execution module as an object, and then sends it to workers when dispatching vertices executing.

To begin the execution, master node first sends the initial vertex to workers. When a worker receives the vertex, its storage component will keep it, and then notifies the registry component through an index publishing message.

Every time the registry component receives an index publishing message for vertex x, it updates x's index and then notifies the dataflow graph component to check if there is a vertex execution waiting x. If so, the ready vertex will be scheduled as an executing task. The scheduling component sends the executing request to candidate workers. The execution request carries the serialized object of corresponding execution module, and the location information of the input vertex data. After receiving it, the worker first fetches the input data, and then un-serializes the execution object and executes it.

To improve the scalability of the system, workers transfer vertex data in a P2P manner. Whenever the executor component receives an executing request from master node, it sends a fetch request to the local storage component. If there is non local copy for the requested data, the storage component will fetch the data from remote worker according to the location specified in the executing request. After all the input data is available on the worker node, the executor component creates a thread instance for the execution module based on the serialized object from the master, feeds it with the input vertices and starts the thread. After the computation finishes, the executor component saves the result vertex into local storage component and notify the registry component.

The storage component keeps hot vertex data in memory while holding cold data on disk. The vertex data will be dumped to disk asynchronously when there is a need to reduce memory space. Worker schedules the executing and network traffic of multiple tasks as a pipeline to optimize the performance.

4.5. Fault Tolerance

In our Desktop Grid environment, besides physical failure (node cannot work due to software or hardware problems), we frequently face soft failure. Soft failure occurs when higher priority users demand node resources and the dataflow system yields. We use same mechanisms handling both failures.

4.5.1. Worker Failure

The *master* monitors status for each task dispatched to workers. Each vertex task has 4 statuses: *unavailable, executing, available* and *lost. Unavailable* and *lost* means no any copy exists in the dataflow storage for the vertex. the difference between these two statuses is *unavailable* is specified to the vertex which is never generated before, while *lost* means the vertex has been generated before but now lost due to worker failures. *Available* means that at least one copy for the vertex is held by some storage component in the dataflow system. *Executing* the vertex has been scheduled to some worker but still not finished.

The failure of a worker/node leads to termination of the task it is processing and the master needs to re-schedule such tasks elsewhere. Furthermore, since the vertex data on the failure worker will not be accessible again, the master node will need to regenerate them if there are some *unavailable* tasks are eventually dependent on them.

When the master detects that a worker has failed, it notifies the registry component to remove the failed worker from indices. During the removing process, status of some of the vertices will change from *available* to *lost*. For the *lost* vertices, if they are directly dependent by some *executing* or *unavailable* vertex tasks, we need to regenerate them to continue the execution. The rescheduled tasks may be dependent on other *lost* vertices, and eventually cause domino effects. For some extreme cases, the master node may need to re-send the initial vertices to continue the execution.

Generally, rescheduling due to the domino effect will takes considerable time. The system replicates vertices between workers to reduce rescheduling. This is a feature triggered by the configuration of the master. If replication feature is set, the registry component will choose candidate workers to replicate the vertex after it receives the first publishing message for that vertex. Replication algorithm needs to take load balancing into consideration.

Replication causes additional overhead. If we take vertices under same version as a checkpoint for the execution, it is not necessary for us to replicate every checkpoint. It is better for users to specify a replication step. It is called as n step replication if users want to replicate the vertices every n versions. Under failure cases, there is a tradeoff between replication steps and executing time.

4.5.2. *Master Failure*

Generally *master* is running over a dedicated node, it may experience physical failures, but seldom has soft failures. To handle this, it frequently writes its internal status, including data structure in registry component, scheduler component and graph component to disk and then replicate the internal status to other node. After the master node fails, we could use the backup version to start a new master and continue the computation.

4.6. Scheduling

In the current design, the scheduling is performed by the master giving priority to locality of data [11] and performance history of workers [17]. For an efficient scheduling, the size of each input vertex data and computing power, i.e. CPU frequency, are taken as the measure for load balancing. The scheduler collects the related performance information for each execution module, such as the input data size and time consumed. Based on this history information, we can predict the execution time for the execution module which has been scheduled.

5. Performance Evaluation

In this section, we evaluate the performance of the dataflow system through two experiments running in a Windows Desktop Grid deployed in Melbourne University and shared by students and researchers.

5.1. *Environment Configuration*

The evaluation is executed in a Desktop Grid with 9 nodes. During testing, one machine works as master and the other 8 machines work as workers. Each machine has a single Pentium 4 processor, 500MB of memory, 160GB IDE disk (10GB is contributed for dataflow), 1 Gbps Ethernet and ran Windows XP.

5.2. *Testing Benchmarks*

We use two examples as testing programs for the evaluation. These examples are built using the dataflow API.

(a) Matrix Multiplication
In this benchmark one matrix is multiplied with another one. Each matrix consists of 4000 by 4000 randomly generated integers. We partition matrix into square blocks with two granularities: 250 by 250 block and 125 by 125 block.

The firs granularity of partition generates 16*16 blocks (255KB per block), and, the second one generates 32*32 blocks (63KB per block).

(b) Matrix Vector Iterative Multiplication

In this benchmark, one matrix is multiplied with one vector in an iterative manner. The matrix consists of 16000 by 16000 random integers, and the vector consists of 16000 random integers. The matrix is about 1GB and the vector is 64KB. The matrix and vector are partitioned by rows. Two granularities for partition are adopted in the evaluation: 24 stripes and 32 stripes.

For 24 stripes, the matrix and the vector are respectively partitioned by rows into 24 pieces. So there are 1200 vertices are generated. For 32 stripes, there are 1600 vertices are generated.

5.3. Scalability of Performance

Figure 3 illustrates the speedup of performance with an increasing number of workers. We can see that under same vertex partition settings as more workers are involved in the computation, better performance is obtained. On the other hand, overheads such as connections with the master also increase with the number of workers. So the speedup line is not ideal.

The matrix vector multiplication benchmark illustrates a super linear speedup phenomenon for one worker. The reason is one computer has only 500MB memory and is not enough to hold 1GB matrix. The swapping overhead causes reduction in performance, where this is not the case with parallelism as data is distributed across multiple workers.

One expectation of partition granularity is that more partitions will introduce additional overhead during execution.

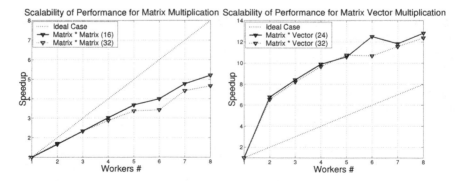

Figure 3: Scalability of performance.

5.4. *Handling Worker Failure*

This section evaluates the mechanisms dealing with worker failure, including replication and rescheduling. We use iterative matrix vector multiplication with 24 partitions and 100 iterations. In total, 2400 vertices are generated during the testing. As vertices created have same size, we measure the vertices number.

8 workers and 1 master involve in the testing. We first collect the number of vertices without worker failures and replication, as the first line in Figure 4. The whole testing lasts for about 4 minutes. Within the initial phase, where the line is nearly flat, the master node sends initial vertices to workers. It is a sequential process. After that, the execution begins and the slope of vertices number line increases heavily. After all vertices are created, the line changes to flat.

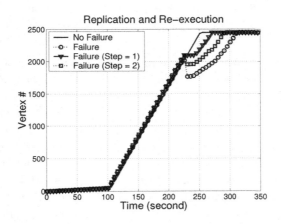

Figure 4: Handling worker failures with replication and re-execution.

Next we add one worker failure in the testing. We unplug one worker's network cable to simulate its failure at around the 4th minute. When we do not take replication, one worker failure causes some vertices to be lost, illustrated by the 2nd line. Once the master detects the failure, it will dispatch live workers to regenerate lost vertices and then continue the execution. So there is a big drop at the 230th second in the 2nd line. After generation of lost vertices, only 7 workers are available, so the slope is smaller than the one before the drop point.

Then we add replication mechanism to handle the failure. We test two settings: 1-step and 2-step replication. Compared with no replication, 2-step replication has only a small drop during the failure while 1 step replication has no drop. Eventually we can see replication mechanism effectively reduces the time consumed for regenerating lost vertices.

6. Conclusion

We presented a dataflow computing platform within shared cluster environment. Through a static dataflow interface, users can freely express their data parallel applications and easily deploy applications in distributed environments. The mechanisms adopted in our system support scalable performance and transparent fault tolerance. We plan to incorporate dataflow model into Alchemi.

Acknowledgments

We would like to thank Yu Chen, Krishna Nadiminti, Srikumar Venugopal, Hussein Gibbins, Marcos Dias de Assuncao, Xingchen Chu and Marco A. S. Netto for their support. This work is partially supported by grants from the eWater CRC and DEST International Science Linkage Program.

References

1. Akshay Luther, Rajkumar Buyya, Rajiv Ranjan, and Srikumar Venugopal. *Alchemi: A .NET-Based Enterprise Grid Computing System.* 6th International Conference on Internet Computing, 2005, Las Vegas, USA.
2. Arvind and R. Nikhil. *Executing a program on the MIT tagged-token dataflow architecture.* IEEE Transaction Computers. 39, 3, 300–318, 1990.
3. David P. Anderson. *BOINC: A System for Public-Resource Computing and Storage.* Proceedings of the Fifth IEEE/ACM International Workshop on Grid Computing, R. Buyya (ed.), IEEE CS Press, USA, 2004.
4. D. Thain, T.Tannenbaum, et al. *Distributed computing in practice: The Condor experience.* Concurrency and Computation: Practice and Experience, 17(2-4), February/April 2005.
5. G. Fedak, C. Germain, et al. *Xtremweb: A generic global computing system.* Proceedings of the 1st International Symposium on Cluster Computing and the Grid (CCGrid 2001), Brisbane, Australia, 2001.
6. I. Foster and C. Kesselman. *The Grid Blueprint for a Future Computing Infrastructure.* Morgan Kaumann Publishers, USA, 1999.
7. J. Dean and S. Ghemawat. *MapReduce: Simplified Data Processing on Large Clusters.* Proceedings of the 6th Symposium on Operating Systems Design and Implementation (OSDI'04), San Francisco, CA, 2004.
8. J.F.Cantin and M.D.Hill. *Cache Performance for Selected SPEC CPU2000 Benchmarks.* Computer Architecture news (CAN), 2001.

9. J. Verbeke, N. Nadgir, et al. *Framework for peer-to-peer distributed computing in a heterogeneous, decentralized environment.* Proceedings of the 3rd International Workshop on Grid Computing, 2002.

10. E. Lee and D. Messerschmmitt. *Static scheduling of synchronous dataflow programs for digital signal processing.* IEEE Transactions Computers. C-36, 1, 24–35, 1987.

11. C. Polychronopoulos and D. Kuck. *Guided self-scheduling: A practical scheduling scheme for parallel supercomputers.* IEEE Transactions on Computers, 36 (12), 1425–1439, 1987.

12. R. Agrawal, T. Imielinski, et al. *Database mining: A Performance Perspective.* IEEE Transactions on Knowledge and Data Engineering, 5(6):914-925, 1993.

13. R.H.Arpaci-Dusseau, Eric Anderson. Noah Treuhaft, et al. *Cluster I/O with River: Making the fast case common.* Sixth Workshop on I/O in Parallel and Distributed Systems, May 5, 1999, Atlanta, GA, USA. ACM, 1999.

14. Rosa M. Badia, J. Labarta, et al. *Programming Grid Applications with GRID superscalar,* Journal of Grid Computing, Volume 1, Issue 2, 2003.

15. S. Bowers, B. Ludaescher, et al. Enabling Scientific Workflow Reuse through Structured Composition of Dataflow and Control-Flow. IEEE SciFlow: The IEEE International Workshop on Workflow and Data Flow for Scientific Application, 2006.

16. S. Altschul, T. Madden, et al. *Gapped BLAST and PSI-BLAST: a new generation of protein database search programs.* In Nucleic Acids Research, pages 3389-3402, 1997.

17. W. Smith, V. Taylor, and I. Foster. *Using Run-Time Predictions to Estimate Queue Wait Times and Improve Scheduler Performance.* Proceedings of the 5th Workshop on Job Scheduling Strategies for Parallel Processing (JSSPP '99), Springer-Verlag, 1999.

18. T.L.Lancaster. *The Renderman Web site.* http://www.renderman.org, 2002.

19. W. M. Johnston, J. R. Hanna, et al. *Advances in Dataflow Programming Languages.* ACM Computing Surveys, 36(1):1–34, March 2004.

20. E. Deelman et. al. Pegasus: a Framework for Mapping Complex Scientific Workflows onto Distributed Systems. Scientific Programming Journal, Vol 13(3), 2005, Pages 219-237.

21. J. Yu and R. Buyya. Scheduling Scientific Workflow Applications with Deadline and Budget Constraints using Genetic Algorithms. Scientific Programming Journal, 14(3-4), 2006, pp. 217 – 230.

PERFORMANCE EVALUATION OF GFARM VERSION 1.4 AS A CLUSTER FILESYSTEM

YUSUKE TANIMURA, YOSHIO TANAKA and SATOSHI SEKIGUCHI

Grid Technology Research Center, National Institute of AIST,
1-1-1 Umezono, Central 2, Tsukuba, Ibaraki 305-8568, Japan.
E-mail: {yusuke.tanimura, yoshio.tanaka, s.sekiguchi}@aist.go.jp

OSAMU TATEBE

Department of Computer Science, University of Tsukuba,
1-1-1 Tennodai, Tsukuba, Ibaraki 305-8573, Japan.
E-mail: tatebe@cs.tukuba.ac.jp

Gfarm was designed and implemented for achieving high scalability of total I/O bandwidth for a comparatively small number of files that have a large file size. In this paper, the performance of Gfarm version 1.4 is measured by both metadata-intensive and data-intensive benchmarks, in order to analyze Gfarm's characteristics in terms of granularity of file operations and file size. The results show a conceivable bottleneck in the use of Gfarm as a cluster filesystem, hints for parameter tuning, and types of applications suitable for use with Gfarm. In our experiment, 5600 files with a file size of 5MB, on average, were created over 112 nodes and read in turn, and a total of 2.2 [GB/sec] for write and a total of 4.2 [GB/sec] for read throughput were achieved.

1. Introduction

Data intensive computing technology is one of the major contributions to science. With recent innovations in grid knowledge and tools, it is practicable to build a petabyte-scale data infrastructure on geographically distributed storage systems. For example, the LHC Grid Computing project at CERN has been distributing raw data to multi-tier worldwide regional centers for permanent back up and data service during the analysis process.[1] The Grid Datafarm architecture was designed for this sort of global petascale data computing.[2] The architecture model specifically targets applications which analyze a set of records or objects independently. The Grid Datafarm takes advantage of this access locality to achieve scalable I/O bandwidth using an enhanced parallel filesystem integrated with process scheduling and file distribution. Gfarm[3] is a reference implementation of the Grid Datafarm and it was previously applied to a high-energy physics application. Performance of distributed file replication on a wide area network was proved to be sufficient at the bandwidth challenge in SC'02.[4]

Since the early-stage implementation of Gfarm, the recent releases of Gfarm, version 1.3 or later, have achieved significant performance improvement in metadata access, and have provided another UNIX command access interface with FUSE.[5] These updates enable Gfarm to be used not only as a global filesystem, but also as a cluster filesystem, meaning Gfarm provides application users a seamless and transparent view from a cluster (LAN-level) system to a grid (WAN-level) system. In order to investigate the practicalibility of using Gfarm as a cluster filesystem, we have measured the performance of the latest implementation of Gfarm, version 1.4, released on November 13 in 2006, using PostMark version 1.5 and the thput-fsys benchmark included in the Gfarm software distribution. In this paper, the basic performance of metadata access and metadata caching is measured, and then the scalability of concurrent access from multiple clients is analyzed with file size parameters. These results help users predict the performance of both metadata-intensive and data-intensive applications in their own scenarios, and reveal for what types of applications they should consider the choice of using Gfarm. If applications run with reasonable access speed to the Gfarm filesystem in the cluster, most of applications can just expand the resource from a cluster to the grid without users' awareness, which is significant for grid applications.

2. Related Work

There are several studies of network shared filesystems that are used for the cluster and have been examined on the grid. Lustre[8] is a high performance parallel filesystem for various kinds of networks, such as TCP/IP, InfiniBand, Myrinet, and so on. In a typical configuration of Lustre, the storage servers are separated from the client nodes, which is unlike Gfarm. Lustre has been demonstrated as a WAN setup among TeraGrid sites in 2006, but there is an issue for lack of WAN level security.

PVFS,[9] which has now moved on to PVFS2, answers a requirement for a fast I/O subsystem from parallel applications. PVFS2 provides a parallel filesystem over a TCP/IP network, as well as on a WAN. File striping, however, must be considered with a network location of I/O nodes. Otherwise file fragment access over a WAN becomes a performance bottleneck.

Compared with those systems, Gfarm implements the X509 public key infrastructure for authentication and encrypted data transfer, and an I/O node selection mechanism with network connectivity in the client library. The I/O performance over a WAN was demonstrated in SC'02.[4] Its performance in a cluster is a remarkable trait for Gfarm.

3. Design of Gfarm Version 1.4

3.1. *Overview and Updates*

Gfarm is a software suite intended to provide the Gfarm filesystem[3] on mainly Linux, but also on FreeBSD, NetBSD, and Solaris platforms. The Gfarm filesystem is a distributed filesystem consisting of local disks of commodity PCs. Multiple PCs in a local area network, compute nodes in a single cluster, multiple clusters in wide area, can all comprise a large-scale and high-performance shared network filesystem when used with Gfarm. Figure 1 shows the components of Gfarm. The Gfarm filesystem nodes (i.e. I/O nodes) provide storage space on their local disks to applications. The Gfarm metadata server manages the metadata of files, I/O nodes, and jobs launched by the Gfarm job invocation method, and answers queries from Gfarm clients. Each Gfarm filesystem node acts as both an I/O node and a client node, which combines to form a single large disk space as the Gfarm filesystem. When a Gfarm client accesses a file by the Gfarm file path, that path must be unique on a Gfarm environment, the client queries the file location from the metadata server. Then the client connects to the I/O node to access the file directly.

The Gfarm filesystem is aimed at data intensive computing that primarily reads one body of large-scale data with access locality. It provides a scalable read and write throughput for large-scale input and output data by integrating process scheduling and data distribution. Without utilizing access locality, a Gfarm application can still access a file, but the I/O will be over a TCP/IP network, which is the same as the method used by a conventional network filesystem.

The latest version of Gfarm is 1.4. The main update from Gfarm version 1.2 to Gfarm version 1.3, or later, is the performance improvement of metadata access. The metadata cache server in Figure 1 is a new component, and it intermediates metadata access between the metadata server and clients. The second important new feature is enhancement of UNIX command access. In addition to the conventional way, which is known as the system-call hook, GfarmFS-FUSE[6] has now become stable, as well. The

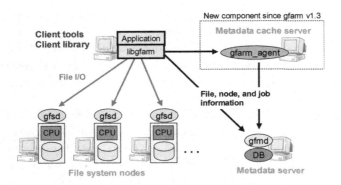

Fig. 1.   Gfarm architecture.

I/O node selection algorithm in the client library has also been improved. The Gfarm client intelligently chooses an I/O node by CPU load, network connectivity, and disk space, where the client then creates a file, or reads a file or its replica from the nearest I/O node. These updates help the use of Gfarm as a cluster filesystem.

3.2. *Improvement of Metadata Access*

Gfarm has supported the LDAP-based metadata server from the beginning. LDAP works slowly, however, when the number of metadata entries is more than 100,000. In order to overcome this limitation, the PostgreSQL-based metadata server has been supported, and a metadata cache server, called *gfarm agent*, has been designed for reducing metadata accesses.

The metadata information for a file consists of 3 parts such as file path, file section and file copy. The directory tree information is generated from path information of all files. On the design of the Gfarm version 1.4, each client needs entire directory tree information to access the Gfarm filesystem. When huge numbers of files are stored on the metadata server, however, the directory tree information is large. In that case, it takes time for the client to retrieve the information from the metadata server. For example, the 'ls' command on the Gfarm filesystem may take several seconds or more. The memory usage is excessive when every client allocates a large amount of memory for the information. By using the gfarm agent, the directory information is cached in the gfarm agent when one client accesses a file, and then that client, or another client, can just look at the cached information, without retrieving the information from the metadata server.

In addition, the gfarm agent can cache file path information in master mode. The master mode drastically improves the file access performance, but only one gfarm agent should be running at a time to keep cache consistency, or users must guarantee that their applications work properly, even if file renaming or creation is not reflected on other gfarm agents during the cache timeout period (1 minute by default).

The gfarm agent is useful in the following cases: when the metadata server is far from the client, the client can use the nearest gfarm agent; when multiple clients read the same files or directories, the client can use cached information. Moreover, to build a larger Gfarm environment for hundreds-of-nodes clusters, we can launch $10 \sim 20$ cache servers to reduce the load on the metadata server.

3.3. *Implementation of UNIX Command Access*

There are two methods used to access the Gfarm filesystem by conventional UNIX command. Both are really useful because application users don't have to rewrite their application programs with the Gfarm API at all. The applications can just open a file on the Gfarm filesystem, and then read, seek or write data with the file, as the file normally exists on the local disk.

As one access method, the Gfarm system-call hook library traps every system-call for file operation. In the case where a file path starts with "*/gfarm*", "*gfarm:*", or "*gfarm@*", an appropriate Gfarm I/O API function is called. The only thing user needs to do to use this method is to set the LD_PRELOAD environment variable.

As the other access method, GfarmFS-FUSE implements an almost fully functional Gfarm filesystem in a userspace program by means of FUSE.[5] On the machines where the fuse kernel module is loaded and the "*fusermount*" command that setuid permission is granted to is installed, users can mount the Gfarm filesystem using the "*gfarmfs*" or "*mount.gfarmfs*" command.

The system-call hook library is implemented simply and it would have less overhead for a single file operation than GfarmFS-FUSE, but more restrictions still remain and developers need to spend more time to update versions. On the other hand, GfarmFS-FUSE has fewer restrictions for file operations, and is easier for a developer to catch up on with a new kernel and a new glibc release. The GfarmFS-FUSE client works faster by caching file path information, the I/O node information, and read/write data, while the I/O bandwidth is lower than that of the system-call hook due to the user-space/kernel-space switch.

Table 1.   Machine specifications.

Metadata server node	CPU: Xeon 2.8 GHz x 2, Memory: 1GB OS: Fedora Core 5 Linux (Kernel version: 2.6.18) Backend DB: PostgreSQL 8.1.4
I/O and client nodes	CPU: Xeon 3.06 GHz x 2, Memory: 4GB Disk: WDC WD2500SB (8KB cache, UDMA/33 mode enabled) OS: RedHat Linux 8.0 (Kernel version: 2.4.24) Filesystem: Ext3

4. Performance Evaluation

Gfarm version 1.4 was evaluated as follows. First, Gfarm's system-call hook library and GfarmFS-FUSE were compared from the performance aspect. Second, the performance of the metadata server and the metadata cache server were measured to see how many transactions they would be able to handle in a second. This result would tell us how we could build hundreds of I/O nodes in a cluster environment. Third, the total throughput of 112 I/O nodes was benchmarked with granularity of file operations.

Table 1 shows the machine specification of our experiments. The disk performance of the I/O node is 29.9 [MB/sec] in device reads and 640 [MB/sec] in cache reads with the *"hdparm"* tool. Use of the gfarm agent depends on each benchmark test. That is to say, the gfarm agent is launched on the metadata server node, launched on some of I/O nodes or not launched.

Two benchmarks, PostMark and the thput-fsys benchmark, were utilized for the evaluation. PostMark is a single-threaded benchmark aimed at measuring filesystem performance over a workload composed of many short-lived, relatively small files.[7] This benchmark can measure the performance of metadata operations. The thput-fsys benchmark which is included in the Gfarm software suite, measures the I/O performance to a single file. It creates a specific sized file with sequential block writes, and then reads the file with sequential block reads.

4.1. *Performance Comparison of UNIX Command Access*

The performance of the Gfarm's system-call hook library and GfarmFS-FUSE was compared with the thput-fsys benchmark and PostMark. The file size parameter of thput-fsys was from 1MB to 8192MB, and the block size for read/write was 8KB. In Table 2 and Table 3, Local is a measurement of the read/write throughput to a local disk. Hook is the measured throughput to the Gfarm filesystem via the system-call hook library. FUSE is the measured throughput via GfarmFS-FUSE, with no options, with buffered mode, with the direct_io option, or with the large_read option. Buffered

Table 2. Sequential block write throughput (Unit: MB/sec).

File size [MB]	Local	Hook	FUSE	FUSE (direct_io)	FUSE (buffered)
1	18.8	9.5	9.8	10.2	9.9
4	24.8	14.7	12.6	13.6	13.2
16	26.0	16.3	14.2	15.2	14.5
64	26.3	17.7	14.6	18.7	15.5
256	26.4	19.2	18.9	19.5	19.0
1024	27.0	26.5	24.2	26.6	25.7
4096	29.2	29.2	26.2	29.1	27.7
8192	30.0	29.7	26.1	29.6	27.6

Table 3. Sequential block read throughput (Unit: MB/sec).

File size [MB]	Local	Hook	FUSE (buffered)	FUSE (direct_io)	FUSE (large_read)
1	1374	33.3	24.6	26.3	27.3
4	1461	41.4	30.2	34.0	36.7
16	1457	44.0	32.4	36.4	39.2
64	1514	44.6	33.1	37.5	40.6
256	1543	44.9	33.5	37.9	40.8
1024	1554	44.9	33.4	38.0	41.1
4096	28.5	28.7	28.7	28.7	28.5
8192	28.5	28.8	28.8	28.7	28.7

mode enables GfarmFS-FUSE to use buffered I/O to the Gfarm filesystem
with a 64KB buffer. The direct_io option disables the use of a file content
cache in the kernel so that the block size specified by applications, 8KB in
this case, is used. The large_read option enables FUSE to issue large read
requests, and hence the block size for read is 64KB. When GfarmFS-FUSE
is started without any options, the block size for read is always 4KB and
the maximum block size for write is 4KB.

From Table 2, the performance degradation of Hook to Local was negligible when the file size was more than 4096MB. The performance of Hook
was equal to FUSE with the direct_io option. FUSE with the direct_io option
achieved the best performance among the 3 options of the FUSE executions.
As shown in Table 3, the read throughput of Local was much higher than
others when the file size was small. The reason is that file consistency is
checked by calculating md5 checksum in the Gfarm library every time the
file is opened. Hook made better performance than FUSE in read. FUSE
with the large_read option was the best among the FUSE executions. When
the file size was larger than memory size, the performance was almost the
same among the five methods.

The basic parameters of PostMark are shown in Table 4. Three sets of
file size range parameters, the minimum size and the maximum size, were
applied to the experiment. In the results shown in Table 6, Hook started
with one of two options and GfarmFS-FUSE started with one of 3 options.

Table 4. Basic parameters of the Post-Mark execution.

Number of transactions	1000
Block size	512 bytes
Number of files	500
Number of subdirectories	50
Read / append ratio	50 % / 50 %
Create / delete ratio	50 % / 50 %

Table 5. Parameters of the PostgreSQL server.

shared_buffer	30,000
max_fsm_pages	330,000
max_fsm_relations	20,000
fsync	off
wal_buffers	32
effective_cache_size	524288
random_page_cost	2

Table 6. Performance comparison in file operations (Unit: tps (number of processed transactions per second)).

File size range	Hook	Hook (path-info cache)	FUSE	FUSE (path-info cache)	FUSE (kernel_cache)
512B – 10KB	50.5	51.9	37.6	44.5	36.8
64KB – 1MB	22.9	25.2	19.0	21.5	22.0
512KB – 10MB	5.66	5.79	3.11	3.13	3.53

The first of both is without any performance-related options, the second is with the "path-info cache" mode, and the last of GfarmFS-FUSE is with the "kernel_cache" option. With the second option of Hook, the PostMark process caches the path and status information of every file during one second. For GfarmFS-FUSE, the GfarmFS-FUSE process does the same. "path-info cache" is the same function as that of using the gfarm agent in master mode. The third enables the kernel_cache option of FUSE. This option disables flushing the cache of the file contents on every open() and it might improve performance in a certain situation, for example, where data is not changed externally.

In Table 6, the result values are the average of 5 trials. Hook can process file operations faster than FUSE. When file path information is cached, the performance improved in both Hook and FUSE. The kernel_cache option was effective when the file size range was from 512KB to 10MB.

To summarize this subsection, Hook works faster than FUSE in both data-intensive access and metadata-intensive access, and the performance of FUSE depends on the option.

4.2. Scalability of Metadata Access

4.2.1. Basic Performance of the Metadata Server and the Gfarm Agent

The PostgreSQL was used as a backend database in this experiment, with tuned parameters shown in Table 5. The performance of our PostgreSQL server was measured by *pgbench*. The pgbench is a simple program used to

Table 7.   Performance of the metadata accesss from one client.

	All transactions	Read only transactions
Direct	49.1	203
Agent (−m) on MS	47.2	193
Agent on MS	38.8	152
Agent (−m) on I/O	48.1	220
Agent on I/O	40.0	177
Client caching	46.4	267

run a benchmark test sort of TPC-B. The local execution result of pgbench on the metadata server was 495 [tps (transactions per second)] in an average of 3 trials, including establishing connections. The pgbench execution on the I/O node to the metadata server was 213 [tps]. When the number of clients increased in the latter case, the performance was saturated around 415 [tps], with 4 clients.

The performance of the Gfarm file operations with the system-call hook, which demonstrated better performance than GfarmFS-FUSE in the previous subsection, was measured by PostMark. The PostMark parameters were the same as those of Table 4 and the file size range was from 512B to 10KB. The result in Table 7 shows the performance with a single client to the metadata server. The case of "All transactions" was measured for all of the create (with write), read, append, and delete operations. The case of "Read only transactions" was only measured for read operations. "Direct" indicates that a client accesses the metadata server without the gfarm agent. "on MS" means that the gfarm agent is launched on the metadata server node. "on I/O" means that the gfarm agent is running on the I/O node. "(−m)" means the gfarm agent runs in master mode. "Client caching" uses Hook with the "path-info cache" mode and accesses the metadata server directly. In these results, path-info cache by using the gfarm agent in master mode or enabling client cache is critical to the performance. The gfarm agent on the client side provides faster access to the metadata than the gfarm agent on the metadata server node.

The execution time of the "ls" command was measured when 1,002,017 files were stored on the Gfarm filesystem. In this case, because the required memory of the directory tree information was 62MB, Hook took 8.2 [sec] to run the "ls" command. Most time was spent retrieving the directory information from the metadata server. When the gfarm agent was used, however, the directory information was cached in the gfarm agent at the first run of the "ls" command, and the second run took only 0.13 [sec]. In addition, only the gfarm agent consumes the amount of 64MB memory for the directory information cache.

4.2.2. *Scalability of the Metadata Access with Multiple Gfarm Agents*

The results in Figure 2 show performance scalability against concurrent metadata access of all kinds of transactions from multiple clients. Every client on every I/O node ran its own PostMark simultaneously. In this figure, "on I/O" means that the gfarm agent is running on every I/O node for the node itself. The result values are an average of 5 trials and the Y-axis shows total transactions of all clients. "Direct" and "Agent on I/O" achieved the same performance in the figure, which means even if the gfarm agent is running on each I/O node, the access speed is limited to the performance of the metadata server. When the path-info cache was enabled in the client, however, the access speed scaled more than that of the direct access. Note that enabling path-info cache might cause cache inconsistency among cache holders. In our experiment, it was not a problem because each benchmark execution used a different scratch directory. "Agent on MS" did not scale because concurrent transactions were queued on the single gfarm agent and processed sequentially.

The benchmark experiment in Figure 2 required a lot of update operations and the cache of the gfarm agent was not very effective. The performance was saturated with more than 6 clients. Therefore, we ran the benchmark with read only operations, and set the parameter for file size to 50 and the number of subdirectories to 5. In 1000 transactions, the same file is referenced 20 times, on average. This result is shown in Figure 3. Compared with Figure 2, "Client caching" in Figure 3 could achieve slightly better scalability.

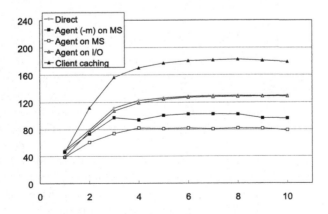

Fig. 2. Scalability of the metadata access of all transactions.

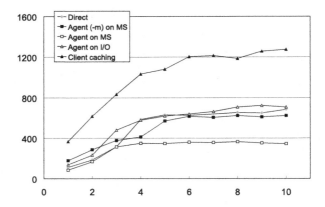

Fig. 3.   Scalability of the metadata access of read-only transactions.

Table 8.   Scalability of the total I/O throughput.

Number of nodes	16	32	48	64	80	96	112
File size range	Read throughput [MB/sec] (average of 5 trials)						
512B–10KB	5.10	6.66	7.42	7.47	7.69	7.20	6.24
64KB–1MB	352	579	714	678	720	698	639
256KB–5MB	613	1203	1773	2237	2600	2766	2820
512KB–10MB	666	1329	1981	2612	3237	3810	4316
File size range	Write throughput [MB/sec] (average of 5 trials)						
512B–10KB	2.09	3.59	3.68	3.52	2.67	3.22	2.38
64KB–1MB	143	326	362	337	241	302	263
256KB–5MB	379	835	1097	1178	1001	1263	1170
512KB–10MB	509	991	1399	1712	2046	2239	2254

4.3. Scalability of the Total I/O Throughput

For analyzing the scalability of the I/O throughput according to file size, we started 112 I/O nodes and 12 gfarm agents. Each gfarm agent managed 8∼10 I/O nodes, that is determined by the results in the previous subsection. One PostMark was launched on every I/O node at the same time, with the parameters of Table 4, but 50 files (and 5 subdirectories). The throughput of read operations and create operations with write is shown in Table 8. In these results, the peak read performance was achieved with 80 nodes and the peak write performance was recorded with 48 nodes, when the file size range was 512B–10KB (the minimum size is 512B and the maximum size is 10KB) and 64KB–1MB. The 256KB–5MB and 512KB–10MB ranges scaled up to 112 nodes for read and the peak write throughput of

256KB–5MB was achieved with 96 nodes. The total throughput was 4.2 [GB/sec] for read, and 2.2 [GB/sec] for write, with 112 nodes, thus each node achieved 38.5 [MB/sec] for read and 20.1 [MB/sec] for write.

5. Discussion

From the performance evaluation in this paper, the system-call hook method is faster than GfarmFS-FUSE in most cases, and GfarmFS-FUSE users need to tune both GfarmFS-FUSE's and FUSE's parameters carefully. The results in Section 4.1 illustrate one way to tune these parameters. Overall, caching file path information is the key to gain scalable performance of metadata access, though there is an issue of cache consistency. If file path information is not cached, the metadata access speed is limited to the performance of the metadata server. This caching can be enabled by the environment variable and the GfarmFS-FUSE's mount option. The gfarm agent is useful for sharing the directory tree information among multiple clients. When the number of files stored on the metadata server is small, the overhead of the metadata access via the gfarm agent is dominant. When huge numbers of files are stored on the Gfarm filesystem, the gfarm agent caches the directory information so that the Gfarm client accesses them with low latency and saves memory usage. As shown in Section 4.3, when file path information is cached and file size is more than 5MB on average, the performance will scale up to 112 clients.

6. Summary

Gfarm uses the access locality to increase the total I/O throughput for data-intensive applications, which is a primary goal of Gfarm. In the meantime, the implementation of Gfarm is not tuned effectively for metadata-intensive access. As a result, the ratio of the metadata access and the I/O throughput in the application is the most important factor in use of Gfarm as a cluster filesystem. This paper reveals numerically acceptable granularity of file size and file-operation frequency in terms of performance scalability, with Gfarm version 1.4. The results include a comparison of two methods of UNIX command access to the Gfarm filesystem, and basic performance of the metadata server and the metadata cache server.

For future work, we would like to compare the performance between Gfarm and other parallel filesystems, such as Lustre[8] or PVFS2.[9] Further performance improvement of the metadata access is being discussed towards development of the Gfarm version 2.x series.

Acknowledgements

We would like to thank to all the members of the Gfarm developer team. Especially, we appreciate contributions of Mr. Nobuyuki Soda (Software Research Associates, Inc.), who is the main programmer of Gfarm, and contributions of Mr. Takuya Ishibashi (SOUM corporation), who is primarily charged with developing GfarmFS-FUSE.

References

1. LHC Computing Grid Project, http://lcg.web.cern.ch/LCG/.
2. O. Tatebe and et al., "Grid Datafarm Architecture for Petascale Data Intensive Computing," Proceedings of the 2nd IEEE/ACM International Symposium on Cluster Computing and the Grid (CCGrid 2002), pp.102-110, 2002.
3. Gfarm, http://datafarm.apgrid.org/.
4. O. Tatebe and et al., "The Second Trans-Pacific Grid Datafarm Testbed and Experiments for SC2003," Proceedings of the International Symposium on Applications and the Internet Workshops (SAINT), 2004.
5. FUSE, http://fuse.sourceforge.org/.
6. GfarmFS-FUSE, http://datafarm.apgrid.org/software/gfarmfs-fuse.en.html.
7. N. Joukov and et al., "Benchmarking File System Benchmarks," Stony Brook University, CS Technical Report FSL-05-04, 2005.
8. Lustre, http://www.lustre.org/.
9. PVFS, http://www.pvfs.org/.

Grid Workflow

TEMPORAL DECOMPOSITION AND SCHEDULING OF GRID WORKFLOW*

FEI LONG

School of Computing
National University of Singapore, Singapore
E-mail: dcslf@nus.edu.sg

HUNG KENG PUNG

School of Computing
National University of Singapore, Singapore
E-mail: dcsphk@nus.edu.sg

Workflow scheduling is a very important system function that Grid systems have to support. But the scheduling of workflow tasks is an NP complete problem. In this paper, we propose a new scheduling method– "temporal decomposition" – which first divides a whole grid workflow into some sub-workflows and then schedules them using a new efficient algorithm. By dividing a large problem (workflow) into smaller problems (sub-workflows), the "temporal decomposition" can achieve much lower computation complexity. Numerical results show that our proposed scheme is more efficient in comparison with a well known existing grid workflow scheduling method.

1. Introduction

The grid workflow has some unique characteristics which are different from conventional workflows, such as business workflow[1]. These characteristics include:

1) Dynamic resources. Unlike in traditional workflow systems, resources in grid network can join and leave the network more dynamically at any time, such as during the execution of associated grid tasks. Such changes of resource quantity if not managed properly may lead to failure of task execution or dead situation.

2) Distributive processing. In conventional workflow systems, resources are normally concentrative and managed centrally. However, both resources and re-

*The work is funded by SERC of A*Star Singapore through the national grid office (NGO) under the research grant 0520150024 for two years.

source management system (RMS) are vastly distributed in grid networks. Thus it is very challenging if not impossible to obtain global resources information for a single request.

3) Indeterministic execution time for tasks. Due to the variance of assigned resource, the execution time for each grid task is uncertain. Furthermore, the capacity of each resource in the grid network is highly diverse, which makes the execution time for the task varying with different assignment of resources. Due to these factors, the conventional workflow management system could not be applied directly to grid environment. A new grid workflow scheduling algorithm is clearly desirable. In this paper, we propose a new distributed workflow scheduling algorithm for grid networks.

It is well known that the scheduling of grid workflow to distributed grid resources is a NP-complete problem. One practical way to tackle such problem is to divide a complex problem into some smaller sub-problems; similar techniques such as the decomposition of workflow is meaningful for solving grid workflow scheduling problem. Besides space decomposition[2] of workflow, which divides the workflow into some parts according to the workflow structure and relationships between tasks, in this paper we present another method to divide grid workflow into smaller parts; it is known as temporal decomposition. Temporal decomposition divides workflow according to the estimated start time of tasks and execution dependencies between tasks.

Our main contributions in this paper are two-folder. First, we introduce a temporal decomposition approach for reducing the NP-hard grid workflow scheduling problem into a simplified tractable sub-workflow (parallel tasks) scheduling problems. Secondly, we propose an efficient on-line scheduling algorithm for decomposed sub-workflow. By using a QoS bid mechanism, this scheduling algorithm can find the near-minimum cost decision without QoS constraint violation.

This paper is organized as follows. In Section 2, we introduce the taxonomy of Grid workflow scheduling and present some existing important grid workflow decomposition and scheduling heuristics. Section 3 presents the system model developed for our proposal. Our proposed solution will be described in Section 4; where as Section 5 evaluates the effectiveness of our proposal through simulation. Finally, we conclude this work in Section 6.

2. Related Work

It is well known that the problem of scheduling parallel tasks to distributed resources is NP-complete. There are many heuristics for obtaining near-optimal solution for such a problem, such as min-min, min-max, genetic algorithm (GA) and simulated annealing (SA), and etc. Besides these heuristics, one possible method to solve NP-hard problem is to divide a big problem into some smaller problems, since the computation complexity decreases dramatically with the problem size. Thus the approach of decomposition of workflow structure is attractive for solving complex grid workflow scheduling problem. There are two different approaches for de-composing workflow– "space decomposition" and "level decomposition"[3]. "Space decomposition" divides the workflow into some parts according to the workflow structure and relationships between tasks. For example, Yu[2] divides workflow into independent branches and synchronization tasks, and schedules these branches or synchronization tasks separately. A synchronization task is defined as a task with multiple preceding tasks or succeeding tasks, while the task with only one or less preceding task and succeeding task is called a simple task. A branch contains a series of simple tasks executed sequentially between two synchronization tasks. The decomposition result of "space decomposition" is highly dependent on the workflow structure. For example, there are many synchronization tasks in a workflow with small number of serial tasks. The scheduling for synchronization task is far from optimal since only one task has been considered.

A simple "level decomposition" method has been proposed by Deelman, et.al.[3]. In such a decomposition method, the abstract workflow is decomposed into some sub-workflows, which consist of tasks with the same level (determined by the execution dependency) in the abstract workflow structure. The new sub-workflow will be submitted to a scheduler, which then makes a scheduling decision based on all tasks in a sub-workflow together instead of individual task. "Level decomposition" is too simple and may not support complicated workflow components, such as looping tasks. Another shortcoming of "level decomposition" is that the next-level sub-workflow will not start to execute until all tasks in previous-level sub-workflow have been completed.

3. System Models

In this paper, we adopt the definition of grid workflow as an abstract representation of application running on grid networks. Grid workflow is a set of tasks that are executed on multi-sited grid resources in a specific pre-defined order[4]. Grid tasks are the atomic level components in the grid workflow. These components are independently executed on the respective local grid resources. The abstract grid tasks may represent various application components, such as MPI tasks which can execute on multiple processors. Thus, these tasks have various QoS requirements, which could be satisfied by proper schedules with appropriate resource allocations. The typical QoS metrics used in grid networks includes[5]: time (deadline), cost (budget) and reliability. As the basic and most important performance metric, "time" refers to the finished time of the whole workflow execution. The usage of grid resources will be charged by the resource owner. Furthermore, the cost of managing workflow in grid system should also be borne paid by the users. The execution of grid tasks depends on the reliability and availability of the resource. For example, when a resource leaves the grid system, all tasks running on it will fail and should be re-executed on another resource.

3.1. *Workflow Model*

The previous work on grid workflow model can be classified to two types– *abstract* and *concrete*. In the *abstract* model, grid workflow is defined without referring to specific grid resources. In the *concrete* model, the definition of workflow includes both workflow specification and related grid resources. Defining a new model for scientific grid application is beyond the scope of this paper. We adopt the abstract DAG model to describe grid workflow as in the following definition.

Definition 1. A grid workflow is a DAG denoted by $W = \{\mathcal{N}, \mathcal{E}\}$, where $\mathcal{N}$ is the set of grid tasks and $\mathcal{E}$ the set of directed task dependencies. Let $s(n)$ and $p(n)$ be the sets of succeeding tasks and preceding tasks of task $n \in \mathcal{N}$ respectively. $n_s \in s(n)$ means $\exists(n, n_s) \in \mathcal{E}$, while $n_p \in p(n) \iff \exists(n_p, n) \in \mathcal{E}$.

In this model, the grid task is an abstract definition, which can be the representation of various categories of tasks, such as data transfer task, computation task and etc.

3.2. *Optimal Objective*

The workflow scheduling problem can be generalized as an integer programming problem, as shown in the following equation.

$$\text{Maximize} \sum_i \sum_j \frac{c_j a_i S_{ij}}{u_j} \tag{1}$$

subject to a time constraint,

$$\sum_j T(a_i, r_j) S_{ij} \leq T_i \tag{2}$$

and a cost constraint,

$$\sum_j C(a_i, r_j) S_{ij} \leq C_i \tag{3}$$

where

$$S_{ij} = \begin{cases} 1, & \text{if } t_i \text{ is assigned to } r_j \\ 0, & \text{otherwise.} \end{cases} \tag{4}$$

In these equations, a_i is the computation amount of task i. u_j and c_j are the utilization and computation revenue of resource r_j respectively. $T(a_i, r_j)$ and $C(a_i, r_j)$ are the execution time and system cost function of schedule (t_i, r_j). Equation (2) shows the execution time of every task should not exceed its time requirement T_i; while Equation (3) specifies that the execution cost of every task also should not exceed its cost requirement C_i. There are some existing algorithms to solve such a integer programming problem[7]. However, all of them have high computation complexities.

4. Our Proposal

4.1. *Maximum Parallel Tasks*

Unlike traditional static scheduling for the whole grid workflow, we introduce the concept of "Maximum parallel tasks" (MPT). The idea behind "MPT" is to solve the NP-complete problem by reducing the problem's size. Besides space decomposition, our approach is based on temporal decomposition which divides workflow according to the estimated start/end time of tasks. The main motivation of temporal decomposition is that usually the time-scale of grid workflow is larger than that of the grid resource variation.

Another idea behind "MPT" is to reduce workflow scheduling problem to parallel tasks (sub-workflow) scheduling. Different from independent parallel tasks, tasks of grid workflow have some inter-dependency, such as execution order relationship and data relevancy. These inter-dependencies make the workflow scheduling more complicated, since the schedule should also satisfy these dependency constraints. Dividing the whole workflow into sets of independent parallel tasks will transform a complex workflow scheduling problem to a simpler parallel tasks scheduling problem.

We use MPT to divide the whole workflow into some parts. Thus the scheduling problem complexity is highly reduced due to the smaller size of MPT compared to that of whole workflow. MPT is defined as the waiting tasks which have no un-started preceding tasks (i.e. all their preceding tasks have been completed or are running), and due for scheduling within the next scheduling window. For example, there are three parallel tasks (task T1, T2 and T3) running in the system, as shown in Figure 1. Task T4, T5 and T6 are the succeeding task of task T1, T2 and T3, respectively. Suppose task T1 finishes before task T2 and T3, and when task T1 finishes, the MPT set will be task T4, T5 and T6, because preceding tasks (T2 and T3) of T5 and T6 are running and the estimated finish times of T2 and T3 do not exceed the scheduling window. Since task T2 and T3 are still running, task T5 and T6 will be scheduled to start after the estimated finish time of their preceding tasks. The main advantage of grid computing is its parallel computation capability. Thus we argue a complex grid workflow should be designed with a large proportion of parallel tasks, in order to better utilize the parallel computation capability in grid environment. Therefore, the size of MPT should not be too small (e.g. equals to 1).

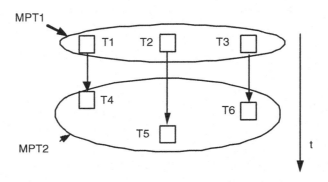

Figure 1.   Example of maximum parallel tasks.

Scheduling window is an important parameter for our system. The size of a scheduling window is the time difference between current scheduling time and next scheduling time. It directly determines the size of MPT waiting to be scheduled. In other words, the size of scheduling window is proportional with the size of MPT. Therefore, it should be neither too small nor too large. The selection of next scheduling time point should consider this aspect. The selection algorithm for the next scheduling time is shown in Algorithm 4.1.

Algorithm 1 Next scheduling time algorithm

$\{f_i\}$ ← finish times of tasks with unscheduled succeeding task(s) in current MPT

e_{min} ← the task with earliest finish time $f_{min} = \min\{f_i\}$

next scheduling time ← e_{min}

Can MPT deal with complicated Grid Workflow components, such as split, merge, condition, loop task? Split component is a Grid task with multiple succeeding tasks; it is fully supported by MPT. When the split task is running or finished, its child tasks (if they have no other preceeding task) can be included in the next MPT and wait for scheduling. The opposite of split component is the merge component which is a Grid task with multiple preceeding tasks. It can be supported by MPT if we add the following constraint: unless all the preceeding tasks of a merge task are running or finished, this merge task can not be scheduled. However, this constraint may impair the performance of the scheduler, since lesser number of tasks in the next MPT could be scheduled. A condition component selects one of the possible next Grid tasks based on a condition. The change of execution path in workflow makes traditional static scheduling schemes not feasible. However, MPT is composed during run-time. It can support condition component well by adding condition constraint. Loop task will be iterated for many times in a Grid Workflow. There are two kinds of loop tasks- fixed loop and condition loop. The iteration times of fixed loop task is predefined and will not change in runtime. Thus we can stretch a fixed loop task to a sequence of tasks which is fully supported by MPT. The condition loop task's execution times depend on a condition expression. By adding the execution condition constraint, MPT can support condition loop task well. We therefore conclude that the MPT can support most of the key workflow components.

4.2. Scheduling Algorithm

The scheduling action is executed in case of following occurrences of events: 1) a new workflow request; 2) the completion of one task; 3) the failure of one task execution or the violation of its QoS tolerance bound. The set of tasks being scheduled in one scheduling action is the set of "maximum parallel tasks" at the scheduling time.

The scheduling algorithm has four steps. First step is to find the set of current "maximum parallel tasks"– T_m. Next is to calculate the execution price $p_{i,j} = \min_i P(i,j)$ for all tasks $t_i \in T_m$, where $P(i,j)$ is the price function of schedule (t_i, r_j). Third is to sort $p_{i,j}$ increasingly and place them in a queue Q_m. Last is to schedule the elements in queue Q_m one by one until the capacity of resource is reached or queue is empty.

Possible scheduling algorithms include genetic algorithm (GA) and simulated annealing (SA). The common shortcoming of GA and SA is their high computation complexity. Here we propose a "minimum-penalty" iterative algorithm. $p_{i,j}$ is the minimum value of all $P(i,j)$. We define "penalty" as following equation,

$$Pen(k,j) = P(k,j) - p_{i,j}, k \neq i \tag{5}$$

The pseudo code of minimum-punish algorithm is shown as Algorithm 2.

Algorithm 2 minimum punish algorithm

1: $n \leftarrow$ number of tasks in T_m
2: **for** $j = 1$ to n **do**
3:    find $p_{i,j}$
4: **end for**
5: check the capacity validness of schedule $\{p_{i,j}\}$
6: **if** schedule $\{p_{i,j}\}$ is valid **then**
7:    **return** optimal schedule $\{p_{i,j}\}$
8: **else**
9:    **repeat**
10:       find resource i_m whose capacity is the mostly violated
11:       find the set of tasks($S(i_m)$) assigned to resource i_m
12:       from $S(i_m)$, find the new schedule (i_n, j_m) with minimum penalty and without new capacity violation
13:       replace schedule (i_m, j_m) with (i_n, j_m)
14:    **until** all resource capacity constraints are satisfied
15: **end if**

---

5. Numerical Results

We evaluated our scheduling algorithm using simulation based on Simgrid2[6] simulation framework. Having been developed by Grid Research And Innovation Laboratory, UC-San Diego, SimGrid and SimGrid2 are the most popular simulation system for Grid scheduling, especially single-client multi-server scheduling in complex and distributed scenario. SimGrid is a discrete event driven system written in C. In SimGrid, the resources are modeled by their latency and service rate, while all actions (computations and communications) are considered as tasks. SimGrid also considers execution time prediction errors to simulate complex situations where execution time cannot be predicted accurately. Both compile time and runtime scheduling algorithms can be simulated by SimGrid. "Compile time" scheduling finishes the schedule before the actual execution, while "runtime" scheduling allows some scheduling decision made during execution. Compared with SimGrid, SimGrid2 has improvements on several aspects, such as more realistic network models and enhanced API. SimGrid2 runs on top of SimGrid and provides users new interface with five fundamental concepts: agents, locations, tasks, paths and channels.

5.1. *Simulation Scenario*

A series of simulation case studies have been performed to evaluate the effectiveness of our new Grid scheduling algorithm. In the first case, we used a small workflow 1 as shown in Figure 2, which consists of ten abstract Grid tasks. The abstract task model contains the computation and QoS requirements of the task; while the resource model has following parameters: computation capability (CPU cycle), capacity, cost and QoS level provided by the resource. The computation capabilities and costs were randomly changed with time. The parameters of workflow example 1 are listed in Table 1. Each task needs different CPU cycles to be completed and different QoS level requirements.

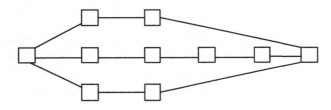

Figure 2.   Workflow Example 1.

Table 1.   Parameters of workflow example 1.

i	1	2	3	4	5	6	7	8	9	10
cycles	50	25	80	50	50	25	80	50	50	25
QoS level	3	2	2	2	1	1	1	2	1	1

The evaluation metrics used in our simulation include makespan (workflow finish time) and cost, which is charged by the resource operator for the usage of the resource. We compared these two metrics exhibited by our MPT scheduling algorithm with that of static and simple level decomposition algorithms.

Besides the simple example workflow 1, we used a more complicated workflow consisting of 128 tasks as workflow example 2. Workflow example 2 consists of three loop tasks, 21 split tasks and 18 merge tasks. Figure 3 shows the makespan result of all three algorithms on two example workflows. Obviously our scheduler has the minimum makespan, while one-by-one scheduler has the greatest makespan. As a static approach, one-by-one scheduler performs the worst in a dynamic grid scenario. In simple level decomposition, the tasks of next level should start after all tasks of current level have been completed. If there is a task A requiring much longer execution time than that of other tasks in current level, there will be a long period with only one task running since the next level tasks cannot start until task A finishes. As shown in Figure 4, our scheduler achieves the lowest cost for both example workflows; while level-decomposition algorithm experiences the highest cost. The result is not surprising since only our scheduler considers the cost in scheduling. Furthermore, the longer the time of their tasks occupying resources, the more the users should pay.

In order to further evaluate the performance of the scheduler more, we used a complex workflow example 3 consisting of thousands of tasks. The simulation results are shown in Figures 5 and 6. Obviously, our scheduler still outperforms both one-by-one and level decomposition algorithms even with a large complex workflow.

Workflow structure is another important aspect which influences the performances of scheduling algorithms, which are based on workflow decomposition. For example, for a workflow consisting of a concatenation of serialized tasks, or a workflow in which all tasks are parallel to each other, simple level decomposition will have the same performance as temporal decomposition. We argue that our scheme is more suitable for complex workflow with large proportion of parallel tasks.

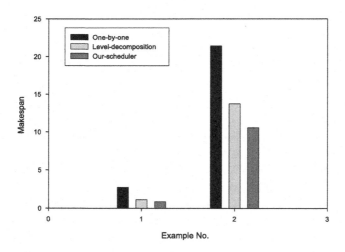

Figure 3. Makespan of example flows.

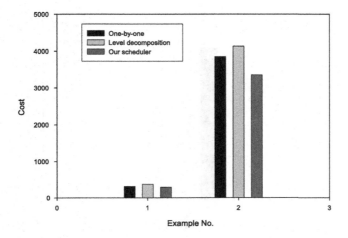

Figure 4. Cost of example flows.

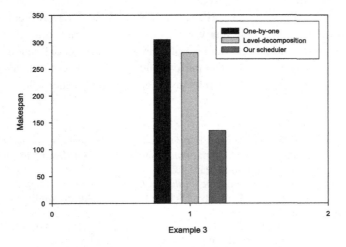

Figure 5. Makespan of example 3.

6. Conclusion

In this paper, we propose a "temporal decomposition" scheme to decouple the whole large workflow scheduling problem to sub-workflow scheduling problem. An added advantage of our scheme is its adaptability to dynamic grid resources.

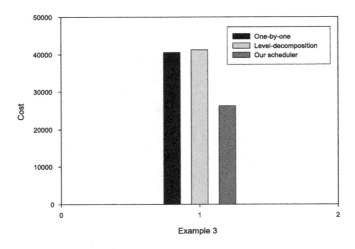

Figure 6.   Cost of example 3.

The sub-workflow schedule is chosen according to the latest states of grid resources, instead of the states at the start time of workflow. We have also developed an scheduling algorithm to solve sub-workflow scheduling problem with resource constraints. The preliminary numerical results demonstrate that our scheme outperforms "one-by-one" and simple "level decomposition" schemes in both makespan and system cost. The performance of our scheduler under grid resource failures is interesting and will be investigated in our further work.

References

1. Shaohua Zhang, Ning Gu and Saihan Li., *Information Technology: Coding and Computing, 2004. Proceedings of 2004 International Conference on.* **Grid workflow based on dynamic modeling and scheduling**, 35 (2004).
2. J. Yu, R. Buyya and Ch. K. Tham, *Proc. of the 1st IEEE International Conference on e-Science and Grid Computing* **QoS-based Scheduling of Workflow Applications on Service Grids**, (2005).
3. Ewa Deelman, James Blythe, Yolanda Gil and Carl Kesselman, etc., *AxGrids 2004, LNCS* **Pegasus: Mapping Scientific Workflows onto the Grid**, (2004).
4. Jia Yu and Rajkumar Buyya, *Journal of Grid Computing* **A Taxonomy of Workflow Management Systems for Grid Computing**, 171 (2005).
5. J. Cardoso, J. Miller, A. Sheth and J. Arnold, *Web Semantics Journal: Science, Services and Agents on the World Wide Web* **Modeling Quality of Service for Workflows and Web Service Processes**, 281 (2004).
6. SimGrid, *http://simgrid.gforge.inria.fr* (2006).
7. Gerard Sierksma, **Linear and Integer Programming, Second Edition** *Marcel Dekker* (2006).

A FLOW MODEL OF WEB SERVICES FOR THE GRID

ENDANG P. SULAIMAN*, YEW–SOON ONG†, MOHAMED S. HABIBULLAH*
and TERENCE HUNG*

*Advanced Computing Programme, Institute of High Performance Computing
1 Science Park Road, Singapore 117528
†School of Computer Engineering, Nanyang Technological University
50 Nanyang Avenue, Singapore 639798

The Grid seeks to provide a universal platform for collaborations among organizations to merge their resources together in a reliable and scalable manner for solving problems that are multidisciplinary in nature. This paper presents a model for representing a problem as a flow based on the semantics of WS–BPEL. In particular, the model permits a link to be declared inside not only a parallel task but also a sequential task. In addition, the concept of normal forms is presented to eliminate ambiguity in the model by regulating the use of links. Several comparisons are also made with a mix of literatures and standards to assess the efficacy of the model itself.

1. Introduction

The convergence with Web Services marks the new era of pervasiveness in the history of the Grid. Web Services [1] define a standard means of interoperating between different applications running on a diversity of platforms. Further, they can be composed in loosely coupled ways to deliver more value-added services off the shelves.

The establishment of Web Services Business Process Execution Language (BPEL) creates the possibility to mix and match services on demand. BPEL [2] defines a grammar to describe the behavior of a process founded on interactions between the process and its partners through Web Services. It is a blend of both graph-structured WSFL [3] and block-structured XLANG [4] that complement each other.

To date, several models have been studied for defining and reasoning about a process. Two examples are Petri nets [5] and process algebra [6]. Verification techniques associated with each model can also be used to ensure that a process behaves correctly. The reader is referred to Ref. 7 for details on numerous works in the related areas.

This paper proposes a model for defining a flow based on the semantics of BPEL. In essence, a flow is a process that allows a link to be declared inside not only a parallel task but also a sequential task. A link inside a parallel task serves to sync between its subtasks whereas a link inside a sequential task serves to skip between its subtasks.

Nonetheless, a flow can grow overly convoluted due to the excessive use of links. If ambiguously applied, a link can cause a flow to behave incorrectly. It is handy, then, to assimilate the idea of normal form by regulating the use of links to eliminate ambiguity in a flow.

The remainder of this paper is organized as follows. Section 2 gives a brief overview of the definition of a flow. Section 3 introduces in details the concept of normal forms. Section 4 presents comparisons with literatures and standards. The conclusion follows thereafter.

2. The Definition of a Flow

In general, a flow comprises a set of tasks that are carried out in a specific order based on their dependencies. Two typical aspects of dependencies that must be supported are task and data dependencies.

Task dependencies are expressed as a task that requires prior carrying out of some tasks. BPEL does support them both implicitly using a *sequence* construct and explicitly using *link*s inside a *flow* construct.

Data dependencies are expressed as a task that requires prior availability of some data. They appear in interactions with another flow as well as variables in the environment. They can also be supported as they are or treated just like any other task dependencies. WSFL supports them using *dataLink* construct whereas XLANG treats them just like any other task dependencies. In BPEL, data can be exchanged with another flow using *invoke*, *receive*, *reply*, and *pick* constructs; as well, data can be exchanged with variables that are declared in the environment using *assign*, *fromParts*, and *toParts* constructs.

The definition of a flow is outlined as follows. A flow F is loosely defined as a 3-tuple:

$$F = (T, L, sf) \tag{1}$$

T is a finite set of tasks, L is a finite set of links, and sf is the F's state. Except for sf, it is easy to see that the definition of a flow rather resembles the definition of a graph, which can lead to a wrong conclusion that a flow is a graph. This is not true generally with regards to both T and L, as explained later.

This simple definition does not, in any way, capture all the requirements of a flow. Certain details, such as *correlationSets*, *eventHandlers*, *faultHandlers*, and *partnerLinks*, are not included as they are not fundamental for the purpose of this paper. Figure 1 shows the state diagram of a flow.

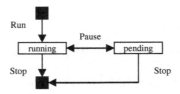

Figure 1. The state diagram of a flow as adapted from WSFL.

Notice that the state diagram defines only two states for the entire lifecycle of a flow, i.e., running or pending. Run, Pause, and Stop operations refer to both human-initiated and machine-initiated operations. Run operation is used by a flow to initiate its execution following an invocation by another flow. Pause operation is used by a flow to defer its execution as it is waiting for some events to happen (e.g., data to arrive, time to elapse, *etc.*) before it can proceed. Stop operation is used by a flow to terminate its execution following both normal and abnormal completions.

The term "task" corresponds closely to the term "activity" in BPEL. A task *t* is defined as:

$$t \in T, t = \left(L^i, L^o, c^j, st\right) \qquad (2)$$

L^i is a finite set of incoming links, L^o is a finite set of outgoing links, c^j is the join condition, and st is the state of t. c^j also corresponds to *joinCondition* construct in BPEL. This definition captures the basic requirements that every type of task should possess. Figure 2 shows the state diagram of a task.

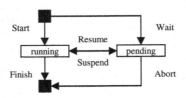

Figure 2. The state diagram of a task as adapted from WSFL.

Observe that the state diagram of a task is analogous to that of a flow. This is because a flow can always be considered as a super task. The only difference is that a task can be pending when initiated. The other operations behave exactly in the same way despite dissimilarities in their names.

The term "link" corresponds closely to the term "link" in BPEL. A link l is defined as:

$$l \in L, l = \left(t^{src}, t^{tgt}, c^{f}, sl\right) \tag{3}$$

t^{src} is a source task, t^{tgt} is a target task, c^{f} is the fire condition, and sl is the state of l. c^{f} also corresponds to *transitionCondition* construct in BPEL. This definition captures the basic requirements that every type of link should possess. Figure 3 shows the state diagram of a link.

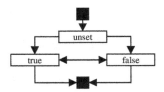

Figure 3. The state diagram of a link as adapted from WSFL.

Observe that the state diagram of a link is tri-state that starts with unset and then resolves to either true or false. Once resolved, a link can still swap its state until the task inside which it is declared has been completed.

As stated earlier, BPEL is a blend of graph-structured and block-structured models, which can be nested and linked in arbitrary ways. Figure 4 shows the set of notations for modeling tasks.

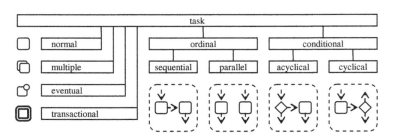

Figure 4. The set of notations for modeling tasks.

These notations are only representative and not exhaustive. They are based on Business Process Modeling Notation (BPMN) with modifications to improve their readability. On further remark, although incomprehensive, it provides some guidelines for mappings to BPEL in the latter part of specifications. The reader is referred to Ref. 8 for more details on the mapping as well as the meaning of each notation. It is necessary to note that XML Process Definition Language (XPDL) is intended to be used as XML representation for BPMN. When required, it can also be loosely mapped to BPEL based on its BPMN depiction.

Of further interests are both ordinal and conditional tasks. Ordinal tasks put importance on the execution order, i.e., sequential or parallel. Conditional tasks are typified by the condition check that happens instantaneously, be it acyclical or cyclical.

Different type of link semantics can be associated with each type of ordinal task. A link inside a sequential task serves to skip between t^{src} and t^{tgt}. Figure 5a demonstrates an example where t_2 will be skipped if c^f of l_a evaluates to true. If false, t_2 will be carried out after t_1. On the other hand, a link inside a parallel task serves to sync between t^{src} and t^{tgt}. Figure 5b demonstrates an example where t_3 will be carried out after t_1 if c^f of l_b and c^j of t_3 evaluate to true. If false, t_3 will be skipped.

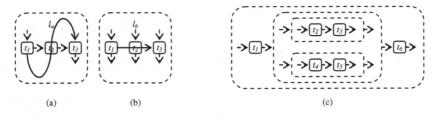

(a) (b) (c)

Figure 5. The set of notations for modeling links.

A flow can be executed by using a regular directed graph traversal algorithm with minor variations to accommodate both nesting and linking tasks. If a task is nested, it is carried out as governed by its super task. On top of that, if a task is linked, it is carried out as governed by its link semantics. A link in a flow is not the same with an edge in a graph. It serves to disrupt a normal path of execution of a flow but it does not generate a new path. Considering this fact, a sequential task can have only a single path whereas a parallel task can have only as many as n paths at a time, where n is equal to the number of its subtasks and greater than zero.

3. The Concept of Normal Forms

The term "normal form" is broadly used in a range of contexts. It usually means the most standard form. The term "normalization" is used to define the process of transforming a thing into its normal form.

To begin with, the idea follows from the classic work in relational database theory [9]. Normalization is applied to eliminate data redundancies and improve data consistencies. In a nutshell, it prevents data anomalies from occurring when performing an operation on a database. In the same way, normalization can also be used to remove ambiguities when performing an operation on a flow. Most of the time, it pertains to the use of links as they are capable of disrupting the path of execution of a flow.

It is important to note that BPEL itself defines a set of regulations governing the link semantics that must be statically enforced. This concept of normal forms is a parallel effort for better standardizing the extension to that link semantics as introduced in this paper.

The 1st Normal Form (1NF) requires that:

(i) Each link must have different t^{src} and t^{tgt}.

(ii) Each link must not have t^{src} that is the same with t^{tgt}.

(iii) Each link must not have t^{src} that encloses t^{tgt}, and *vice versa*.

These requirements are exactly the same with what defined in BPEL. They are devised to validate both the source task and the target task of a link. The first requirement entails each link to be distinctive in terms of its pair of source task and target task. The second requirement entails each link to have its source task that is not the same with its target task. The third requirement entails each link to have its source task that does not enclose its target task, and *vice versa*. The term "enclosure" denotes a hierarchical relationship between two tasks where a super task always encloses its subtasks. Besides what listed above, some prerequisites are assumed to hold true for these requirements to be enforced and, thus, never mentioned properly, e.g., both t^{src} and t^{tgt} must not be empty, c^f must be defined, *etc.*

1NF provides a starting point in standardizing the link semantics. It ensures that each link is unique and both its source task and its target task are identified as unambiguously as possible. Even so, there is always likelihood that the list is not complete. In consequence, more requirements can always be added into the list as deemed appropriate.

The 2nd Normal Form (2NF) requires that:

(i) A flow meets all of the requirements of 1NF.
(ii) A link must be declared inside an ordinal task.
(iii) A link must not cross the boundary of a conditional task.

By being declared, it means that the nearest common super task of both the source task and the target task of a link must be the ordinal task itself. Let s-link be a link that is declared inside a sequential task and p-link a link that is declared inside a parallel task. Recall from figure 5 that both s-link l_a and p-link l_b run the risk of skipping a task from being carried out. Problems will occur if the task that gets skipped is the source of a p-link, the target of which can never be running as its state is never resolved.

This is when Death-Path-Elimination (DPE) proves useful. BPEL spells out that DPE has the effect of propagating false state transitively along succession of p-links until a task is reached with c^j that evaluates to true. However, DPE is not needed in the case of an s-link as it involves only a single path at a time. On the contrary, a p-link involves two paths at a time. If the source task gets skipped, it means that the dependency is missed and the target task can never be carried out if DPE is not in place.

To impose consistency, a link must not cross the boundary of a conditional task. Its subtasks may be carried multiple times or not be carried out altogether depending on its condition as evaluated during runtime. However, this limitation can be overcome by replacing the condition imposed in conditional task with an s-link. Some examples are given later.

The 3rd Normal Form (3NF) requires that:

(i) A flow meets all of the requirements of 2NF.
(ii) An s-link must not cross the boundary of a parallel task.

As said earlier, an s-link is declared inside a sequential task. However, some parallel tasks can be nested in a sequential task to inject concurrencies. An s-link must not cross the boundary of a parallel task even if it still follows 2NF. Using figure 5c as an example, suppose there are two s-links declared from t_1 to t_3 and from t_4 to t_6. If c^f of the former evaluates to true, will t_4 and t_5 also be carried out since they are parallel with t_3. If c^f of the latter evaluates to true, will t_6 also wait for t_2 and t_3 since they are parallel with t_4. Moreover, the situation exacerbates if two or more s-links leave the boundary of a parallel task simultaneously, which can potentially result in state explosion.

The 4th Normal Form (4NF) requires that:

(i) A flow meets all of the requirements of 3NF.
(ii) A p-link must not form a cycle with other p-link(s).

Strictly speaking, it is perfectly all right for an s-link to create a cycle. This requirement is in place only to eliminate a cycle that is accidentally created by a p-link, which will definitely cause a deadlock. This is in line with what is defined in BPEL. Specifically, the source task of a p-link must not have the target task as a logically preceding task. Using figure 5c as an example, suppose there are two p-links declared from t_3 to t_4 and from t_5 to t_2. For t_2 to be carried out, it requires t_5, which requires t_4, which requires t_3, which in turn requires t_2 to be carried out in advance.

When evaluating BPEL's support for normalization, it is imperative to know that it does not impose in itself the hierarchical requirements. Consequently, the first requirement of each NF, except 1NF, is dropped and the results are given in Table 1. '+' means supported and '-' means not supported.

Table 1. The evaluation results of BPEL's support for normalization.

No.	Normal Form	BPEL
1.	1NF	+
2.	2NF	+/-
3.	3NF	-
4.	4NF	+

1NF and 4NF are supported by BPEL because it defines the use of p-links in its specifications. 2NF is partially supported and 3NF is not supported by BPEL because it does not define the use of s-links as introduced in this paper.

If a task is the source of multiple s-links, at most one s-link can fire. On the contrary, if a task is the source of multiple p-links, more than one p-link can fire. Furthermore, c^j is evaluated at the earliest time possible. This is not the case with BPEL as it defers the evaluation until the states of all p-links of which the task is their target are determined.

In addition to that, BPEL defines that a p-link must not cross the boundary of a cyclical task. This is because a p-link will get reevaluated too frequently due to the recurring nature of a cyclical task. However, it is not regulated into one of the NF since it does not pose any ambiguity. Only when a task is repeated, then the states of all links declared inside it will be unset and reevaluated, otherwise they will just be reevaluated.

4. Comparisons with Other Works

Aalst *et al.* [10] gives a thorough analysis on 20 flow patterns that are commonly used in designing a flow, as approached purely from the practical fronts. Table 2 lists down all of the patterns.

Table 2. The list of 20 flow patterns as described in Ref. 10.

No.	Pattern	No.	Pattern
1.	Sequence	11.	Implicit Termination
2.	Parallel Split	12.	MI[1] without synchronization
3.	Synchronization	13.	MI[1] with *a Priori* Design Time Knowledge
4.	Exclusive Choice	14.	MI[1] with *a Priori* Runtime Knowledge
5.	Simple Merge	15.	MI[1] without *a Priori* Runtime Knowledge
6.	Multi-Choice	16.	Deferred Choice
7.	Synchronizing Merge	17.	Interleaved Parallel Routing
8.	Multi-Merge	18.	Milestone
9.	Discriminator	19.	Cancel Activity
10.	Arbitrary Cycles	20.	Cancel Case

[1] MI = Multiple Instances

Supports for pattern 1–7 are straightforward by combining both ordinal and conditional tasks together. Pattern 8 is not supported since it deals with multiple executions in the same path, which can lead to state explosion. Yet, Pattern 9 is supported by evaluating c^j at the earliest time possible if n-out-of-m p-links have evaluated to true. Pattern 10 is supported by declaring s-links inside a sequential task.

Further down the list, pattern 11 is supported due to the fact that a flow will terminate once all tasks have completed. Pattern 12–15 are supported by making use of a multiple task. In particular, Pattern 15 requires a common variable to be used to keep track the number of tasks that have been instantiated so far. Pattern 16 is supported by making use of an eventual task to defer the decision between several paths to be as late as possible. Pattern 17 is supported by making use of a transactional task in a parallel task with a key that is shared mutually among all of them. Pattern 18 is supported by using *eventHandlers* construct in BPEL. In this case, each task can have its inner handler to take care of the internal events and share the outer handler to take care of the external events. Pattern 19–20 are supported by using the `Stop` and `Abort` operations to terminate the execution of a task as well as the entire flow.

74

Below is an example of Hierarchical Parallel Genetic Algorithm using Grid computing, described in Ref. 11. Figure 6a shows one result done not using any link whereas figure 6b shows another result done using links.

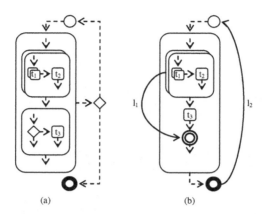

Figure 6. A flow of Efficient Hierarchical Parallel Genetic Algorithms as described in Ref. 11.

t_1 refers to the evaluation of the objective function, t_2 refers to the common operators of Genetic Algorithm, i.e., selection, crossover, and mutation, t3 refers to the migration operator between populations in GA. Both conditional tasks that are present in figure 6a can be easily replaced with l_1 and l_2. Those circles refer to the start, intermediate, and end of a flow, see Ref. 8. Moreover, another task can be introduced parallel with both t_1 and t_2 for visualizing the in-between results as a means of feedback.

5. Conclusion

This paper investigates a model for defining a flow that extends the semantics of BPEL by allowing a link to be declared inside not only a parallel task but also a sequential task. The idea of normal forms is presented to eliminate ambiguity in the model due to the improper use of links. Comparisons show that the semantics enable some advanced flow patterns to be expressed neatly in the model.

Acknowledgments

This work is funded by the A*STAR SERC Grant numbered 0520150024 for the Grid-based Problem Solving Environment for Engineering of Materials.

References

1. Web Services Architecture Working Group, *Web Services Architecture*, W3C Working Group Note, 11 February 2004.
2. Web Services Business Process Execution Language Technical Committee, *Web Services Business Process Execution Language Version 2.0*, OASIS Public Review Draft, 31ˢᵗ January 2007.
3. F. Leymann, *Web Services Flow Language*, IBM Corporation, 2001.
4. S. Thatte, *XLANG: Web Services for Business Process Design*, Microsoft Corporation, 2001.
5. C.A. Petri, "Kommunikation mit Automaten", *New York: Griffiss Air Force Base, Technical Report RADC-TR-6--377*, vol. 1, pp. 1-Suppl. 1, 1966.
6. R. Milner, *A Calculus of Communicating Systems*, Springer-Verlag, 1980.
7. F. van Breugel and M. Koshkina, "Models and Verification of BPEL", *draft*, September 2006.
8. Business Process Management Initiative, *Business Process Modeling Notation Specification*, OMG Final Adopted Specification, 6ᵗʰ February 2006.
9. E.F. Codd, "A Relational Model of Data for Large Shared Data Banks", *Communications of the ACM*, 13(6), pp. 377-387, June 1970.
10. W.M.P. van der Aalst, A.H.M. ter Hofstede, B. Kiepuszewski, and A.P. Barros, "Workflow Patterns", *Distributed and Parallel Databases*, 14(1), pp. 5-51, July 2003.
11. D. Lim, Y.S. Ong, Y. Jin, B. Sendhoff, B.S. Lee, "Efficient Hierarchical Parallel Genetic Algorithms using Grid Computing", *Future Generation Computer Systems: The International Journal of Grid Computing: Theory, Methods and Applications*, 23(4), pp. 658-670, May 2007.

A COMPARISON STUDY BETWEEN DISTRIBUTED AND CENTRALIZED JOB WORKFLOW EXECUTION MODELS

YUHONG FENG and WENTONG CAI

School of Computer Engineering
Nanyang Technological University, Singapore 639798
E-mail: {yhfeng, aswtcai} @ntu.edu.sg

Job workflow execution can be classified into *centralized execution* and *distributed execution*. The centralized execution may cause problems such as single point of failure and poor scalability; whereas the distributed job workflow execution may bring additional runtime overhead. This paper describes a comparison study between these two execution models. First, to put discussion into prospective, our framework for mobile agent based distributed job workflow execution over the Grid: *Mobile Code Collaboration Framework* (MCCF) is described. Second we introduce a commonly used centralized execution engine, Condor DAGMan. Then, the differences between job workflow execution in our context and those in the Condor DAGMan are discussed. Finally, a comparison study using simulated job workflows executed on a prototype implementation of the MCCF and Condor DAGMan is carried out on an emulated WAN setup. The results show that MCCF achieves better job workflow execution time.

1. Introduction

Data intensive scientific applications, such as bioinformatics [16], often involve diverse, high volume, and distributed data sets. They can be generally expressed as a workflow of a number of analysis modules, each of which acts on specific sets of data and performs multidisplinary computations.

During the course of a job workflow execution, a control thread is the thread that manages the data dependency between subjobs, selects resources for ready subjobs, and enacts the subjobs' executions. According to how many control threads are used and where the control threads are executed, the job workflow execution can be classified into *centralized execution* and *distributed execution*. When the centralized execution is used, there is only one control thread and the control thread is fixed on a certain computational resource. The control thread handles all the *control messages* during the job workflow execution. The control messages are the messages communicated to instruct the receiver to take actions. Existing scientific workflow engines such as Condor's DAGMan (DAGMan for short)[a] and SCIRun[b] support centralized job workflow execution.

When distributed execution is used, there can exist multiple control threads and the control threads are deployed on distributed computational resources. Multiple control threads manage the control messages for data independent subjobs, which can improve the system performance. Therefore, research works have been carried out to develop distributed workflow execution using *collaborative engines* [19] or *mobile agents* [2]. When collaborative engines are used, the subjob executions in a job workflow are not handled by a centralized engine, but by multiple distributed engines collaboratively. These engines are instantiated on distributed computational resources and share the same job workflow specifications. They independently or collaboratively select the resources, control the executions for the subjobs that they are responsible for.

Mobile agent is a program which is capable of migrating from one computational resource to another, performing computations on behalf of the user [1]. Mobile agent based job workflow execution is another paradigm for distributed job workflow execution. In data intensive scientific computations, the size of the computation code can be assumed to be less than that of the required distributed data sets [5]. Therefore, moving code instead of data can help reduce the data transmission over the network. The Mobile Code Collaboration Framework (MCCF) is developed to support mobile agent based distributed job workflow execution [11]. Different from the exiting mobile agent based job workflow execution [2], in MCCF, executable codes are provided as dynamic services, i.e., executable codes can be downloaded and instantiated on arbitrary computational resources. Light-weight Mobile Agent (LMA) [6] and Code-on-Demand (CoD) [15] techniques are adopted in the development of the MCCF, so that an analysis module in data intensive scientific applications can be executed at a computational resource close to where the required data set is.

Centralized execution can make the centralized server the system bottleneck. However, mobile agent based distributed job workflow execution brings additional runtime overhead for agent migration, dynamic instantiation, and execution coordination. Hence, the objective of this paper is to compare these two workflow execution models by studying the MCCF and the DAGMan.

---

[a]http://www.cs.wisc.edu/condor/dagman/
[b]http://software.sci.utah.edu/scirun.html

2. MCCF

2.1. *MCCF Overview*

Assuming that executable codes are kept in code repositories to provide dynamic services, Grid resources then include data repositories, computational resources, code repositories, and network resources. Initially, the job workflow specification in the MCCF is abstract (i.e., the computational resources to execute subjobs, locations of data sets, and location of code to be executed for subjobs are not specified). The objective of the MCCF is to map the abstract job workflow provided by users to the Grid resources dynamically for distributed job workflow execution, as shown in Figure 1.

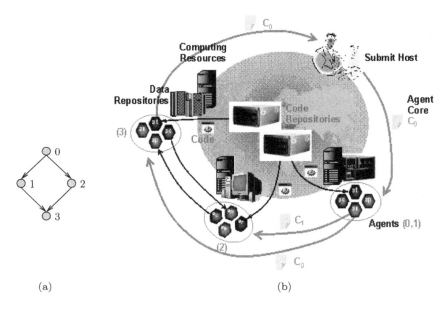

(a)   (b)

Figure 1.   MCCF Overview

LMA is used in the MCCF for the purpose of separating the functional description and the executable code. The functional description is described using *Agent Core* (AC). An AC is essentially an XML file, containing the job workflow specification and other necessary information for agent creation and execution. An AC can be migrated from one resource to another. As for the executable code, to separate subjob specific code and common non-functional code (i.e., the code for handling resource selection, subjob execution, agent communication, and AC migration), CoD is used in the MCCF, that is, subjob specific code is downloaded to the computational resource and executed on demand. The execution of common non-functional codes is carried out by a group of underlying *AC agents* (or agents in short). These agents are temporary and local to the computational resource on which they are running. They are constructed on the computational resource when an AC arrives and destructed when the AC is migrated or discarded. The AC agents include *schedule agent* (as), *task agent* (at), *partner agent* (ap), and *coordination agent* (ac).

An AC may be responsible for the execution of a group, but not all, of subjobs. Upon the completion of a subjob's execution, the AC will be updated with the location of the subjob's execution result before it is migrated to execute the next subjob. When multiple data independent subjobs can be executed concurrently, replicas of an existing AC will be generated so that there is one AC for each subjob. The ACs will then be migrated to the different computational resources for the execution of these data independent subjobs in parallel. When multiple concurrently executing subjobs have a common immediate successor, only one of the corresponding AC replicas should be selected for the latter's execution. Others should be discarded if they are not migrated to any successor's execution.

A job workflow can be graphically represented as a DAG, where the vertices represent subjobs and directed edges represent data dependency between subjobs. It is assumed that a DAG representing a job workflow always has a unique staring node and a unique end node. An AC will be created by the submit host, and the same AC will be migrated back to the submit host with final result after the job workflow completes its execution.

One possible scenario of the distributed execution of job workflow illustrated in Figure 1 (a) is shown in Figure 1 (b). Assuming that subjob 0's corresponding AC replica is denoted as C_0, after subjob 0 completes its execution, subjobs 1 and 2 are ready. A replica of the original AC, denoted as C_1, needs to be created. These two AC replicas are then migrated to their selected computational resources for subjob execution simultaneously, as illustrated in Figure 1 (b). The selection of the computational resource could be based on the load situation of resources or the cost of the computation, depending on the specified user preference.

Similarly, after subjobs 1 and 2 complete their executions, the resources for the execution of subjobs 3 are scheduled. For this particular example, subjob 3 is the end node, therefore, one of the AC replica, suppose it is C_0, will be migrated back to the submit host. Meanwhile, C_1 will be discarded.

2.2. System Design and Implementation

The MCCF system design consists of *built time functions* and *runtime functions*. The built time functions include functions for the AC construction. The user uses the *job workflow editor* to generate the job workflow specification, which is processed by the *AC constructor* to generate an AC. The runtime functions consist of two parts: *Pre-installed functions* and *dynamically generated functions*. The Pre-installed functions are always running in a candidate computational resource, and they are responsible for managing the migration of an AC (which is carried out by the *AC dispatcher*), receiving an AC and instantiating the corresponding AC agents (which are carried out by the *AC receiver*). The dynamically generated functions are carried out by the AC agents. The functions consist of subjob execution, subjob resource selection, execution coordination [14], provenance recording and collection [13]. Globus toolkits are used for accessing resources on the Grid and for data transmission between the resources. The components for distributed job workflow execution in MCCF and their relationship are illustrated in Figure 2.

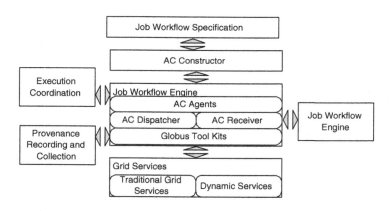

Figure 2. MCCF Architecture

We have built a simple prototype of the MCCF to illustrate the distributed job workflow execution over the Grid. Our implementation is built using J2ME (Java 2 MicroEdition) and JADE [3]. Java is chosen as the implementation language for the following two reasons: (i) it is platform-independent; and (ii) its customerized ClassLoader and inspection mechanism make dynamic class loading possible. Java CoG-1.1 [4] is utilized to access Grid services. Globus2.2 needs to be installed on each selected computational resource. A delegator based execution coordination mechanism [12, 14] and a decentralized provenance recording and collection algorithm [13] have been adopted in the MCCF to support dynamic AC replication and migration.

AC agents are implemented by extending the JADE agent class. For simplicity, resources for subjob execution are selected randomly on runtime. A simple code repository service is implemented as proof-of-concept. Java byte codes are provided at a specified resource, acting as code repository. Data sets are stored as files, on a specified resource, acting as data repository. Gridftp is used to download the codes, fetch the required data sets and transfer the AC replicas between the selected resources.

3. Job Workflow Execution on DAGMan and MCCF

Condor Directed Acyclic Graph Manager (DAGMan) is a commonly used Grid-based workflow execution engine. Condor [8] is a specialized resource management system, which constructs distributed high-throughput computing facility by collecting distributively owned workstations and dedicated clusters. Condor-G [9] is a grid enabled version of Condor, which augments the Globus toolkits with a reliable job submission mechanism. Condor DAGMan uses the centralized model to manage the execution of a job workflow and uses Condor or Condor-G to enable the job execution on the cluster or Grid environment respectively. Normally, the submission host schedules and coordinates the execution of subjobs, and stages the executable codes to the scheduled computational resources for execution. In addition, the submit host also manages the data transfer between computational resources.

The workflow specifications submitted to DAGMan are concrete workflow specification, which require physical locations of input/output data, executable codes, and execution platforms. For a given job workflow, there is one general DAGMan submit file that defines all subjobs, the subjob data dependencies and the tasks to be executed before a subjob's execution ("PRE" scripts) or after a subjob's execution ("POST" scripts). "PRE" or "POST" scripts can be used to stage the required data in or out the execution host. However, these scripts are executed by the submit host, although data are transferred between the execution hosts directly. For each subjob there is a condor submit description file, which specifies the operations to be performed on the given remote machine.

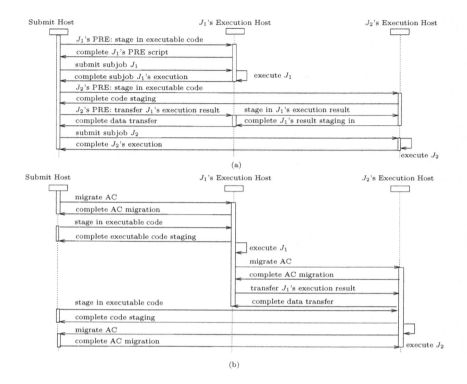

Figure 3.   Workflow Execution over DAGMan and MCCF

DAGMan supports centralized job workflow execution; whereas the MCCF supports distributed job workflow execution. Figures 3 (a) and (b) illustrate that a simple job workflow, which consists of two subjobs j_1 and j_2 with j_2 dependent on j_1, is executed using the DAGMan and the MCCF respectively. As illustrated in Figure 3 (a), for the DAGMan, the submit host acts as the centralized server, which manages the data dependency between subjobs, stages the required executable codes and data sets in the selected execution host, manages the transfer of intermediate results between execution hosts, and submits the subjob execution to the remote execution host. All the control messages are handled by the submit host. In comparison, Figure 3 (b) illustrates the same job workflow executed by the MCCF. To be fair, the submit host is assumed to act as the code repository. Figure 3 (b) shows that the control messages for MCCF are distributed on all execution hosts during the job workflow execution.

From Figures 3 (a) and (b), it is easy to see that there are almost the same number of control messages over the network during the job workflow execution in DAGMan as that in the MCCF. When there are multiple data independent subjobs, AC replications are created in the MCCF, the control messages for these subjobs's execution will be managed by several group of distributed AC agents simultaneously. However, in the DAGMan, all the control messages for the execution of the data independent subjobs are handled sequentially. This makes the submit host the system bottleneck.

However, the MCCF brings additional runtime overhead: (i) the overhead caused by AC migration; (ii) the delay caused by AC agents constructed on each host on AC arrival; and (iii) the overhead for execution coordination. To evaluate the performance of the MCCF and the DAGMan, an experimental study is carried out to compare the makespan of the simulated job workflow execution over the MCCF and the DAGMan.

4. Performance Evaluation

4.1. *Testbed Configuration*

Grid based distributed computation is usually carried out on WAN rather than on LAN clusters. To emulate the network characteristics over the Grid, the ModelNet [17], which emulates WAN network delivery characteristics on a LAN clusters, was used.

Our ModelNet setup consists of 17 machines, one of which runs the emulator and the others host virtual nodes. A network topology used in the WAN emulation experiment was generated by inet [18] using the transit-stub model. It consists of 4000 nodes. 17 clients, which run on the virtual nodes, were created. They were randomly attached to the stub domains in the generated network topology. The link delay is set based on the length of the link and the link bandwidth. There are four types of links in transit-stub model (i.e., client-stub, stub-stub, stub-transit, and transit-transit links). Their bandwidths are given in Table 1.

The MCCF prototype system and the DAGMan were deployed to the emulated WAN using the ModelNet. One machine runs as submit host. Except for the emulator, all other 16 machines are installed with Globus2.2 and Personal Condor 6.6.1 or Condor 6.6.5 using Condor's default configuration. Resource scheduling may have effect on job workflow execution. However, resource scheduling is not the research focus of this paper. In order to avoid the undetermined factors that may affect a job workflow execution time, the machines are dedicated for our use during our experi-

Table 1. Link Characteristics in the
Emulated WAN.

Type of Links	bandwidth
client-stub	100Mbps
stub-stub	10Mbps
stub-transit	10Mbps
transit-transit	100Mbps

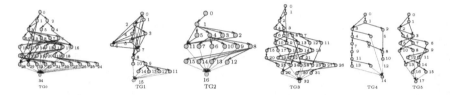

Figure 4. Random Task Graphs

ments and the resources for each subjob execution are predetermined. The objective of the experiment is to evaluate the benefit/cost of distributed job workflow execution in terms of the number of control messages and control threads generated to handled the control messages.

4.2. *Simulated Job Workflow*

We generated 6 psudorandom TGs using the Task Graphs for Free (TGFF) system [10]. Since in our discussion, we assume that there is a unique end node for every TG, when a TG has multiple subjobs that have no offspring, a hypothetical subjob, also referred to as end node, is added. This subjob serves as their common immediate successor to consolidate the final results and has no computation cost. The generated TGs are illustrated in Figure 4, where the dotted, filled circle denotes the added hypothetical subjob, and the dotted edge denotes the added edges.

Each subjob in the workflow executes the same executable file and generates a 28000-byte output file, which is the input of its successors (if any). Since the objective is to evaluate the overhead of control messages and communication messages transmission over the newtork, it is important to vary the complexity of the topologies of job workflows. What each subjob executes is not really relevant.

4.3. *Experiment Results*

The number of control threads (in the MCCF, this is equal to the number of AC replicas), the number of control messages sent over the network, the maximum number of messages handled by an engine[c], and the makespan of each simulated job workflow are shown in Table 2. In addition, Table 2 also shows the percentage improvement of the makespans of the job workflows executed on the MCCF over that on the DAGMan. From these results, we observe that:

Table 2. Performance Evaluation on DAGMan and MCCF.

TG	# of task		# of Control Threads		# of Control Messages			Makespan (s)		
ID	DAGMan	MCCF	DAGMan	MCCF (# of AC)	DAGMan (on submit host)	MCCF per AC agent	overall	DAGMan	MCCF	% Improvement
TG0	33	35	1	22	246	34/86%	248	2346	1795	23 %
TG1	14	16	1	6	120	14/88%	122	2660	1906	28 %
TG2	15	17	1	11	114	18/84%	116	1259	991	23 %
TG3	31	33	1	11	218	18/92 %	220	2471	1571	36 %
TG4	13	15	1	5	88	10/89 %	90	1988	1174	41 %
TG5	16	18	1	6	114	10/91 %	116	1510	1160	23 %

- On the MCCF, there can be multiple control threads, i.e., multiple AC replicas, for job workflow execution. However, on the DAGMan, there is always only one centralized control thread. When there are multiple data independent subjobs ready for execution, multiple control threads can handle the control messages for these subjobs' execution concurrently, which can improve the job workflow execution time.
- Compared with the condor, the distributed job workflow management in the MCCF requires two additional control messages to return the original AC to the submit host. However, the maximum number of messages handled by an AC agent in the MCCF is much less than that in the DAGMan, the improvement ranges from 84% to 92% for the task graph used in the experiments. All the control messages are handled by the submit host in DAGMan makes the DAGMan the system bottleneck.

In all, because of the distributed nature of Grid resources, for a large job workflow, there can be a non-negligible overhead involved in sending the control messages over the network for the centralized model. In addition,

---

[c]An engine refers to the AC agents in the MCCF, and the DAGMan on the submit host in the DAGMan.

by decentralizing and parallelizing the management of the control messages using light weight mobile agent technology, the MCCF achieves better job workflow makespan than the DAGMan, the improvement is 23 % to 41 % for the task graph used in the experiments, as shown in Table 2.

5. Conclusion

Data intensive scientific applications can be generally expressed as a workflow of a number of analysis modules. The centralized job workflow execution may cause problems such as single point of failure and poor scalability. Mobile Code Collaboration Framework (MCCF) supports the distributed job workflow execution. Lightweight Mobile Agent (LMA) and Code on Demand (CoD) technologies are used in the construction of the MCCF. LMA in the MCCF is defined using Agent Core (AC). AC is like a "blueprint" [7]. It is migrated amongst computational resources. Agents are created on its behalf and carry out the required work. AC may also be replicated when necessary.

There is no centralized server in the MCCF. However, It brings additional runtime overhead, e.g., the overhead caused by AC migration and the delay caused by AC agents constructed on each host on AC arrival. By studying a job workflow execution over the MCCF and the DAGMan, we first analyzed the benefits and costs of distributed job workflow execution. Then, we carried out an empirical comparison study on these two workflow engines using the simulated job workflows. The experiment results show that the MCCF achieves better job workflow execution time.

In our experiments, we studied the benefit/cost of distributed job workflow execution in terms of the number of control messages and control threads generated to handled the control messages in this paper. In fact, resources for the execution of data independent subjobs can be selected by distributed agents concurrently during the course of a distributed job workflow execution. In our future work, we will further investigate how this distributed subjob resource selection may affect the overall system performance.

References

1. Ajanta Mobile Agents Research Project. `http://www.cs.umn.edu/Ajanta/`.
2. Bioagent. http://www.bioagent.net/.

3. Java Agent Development Framework. `http://sharon.cselt.it/projects/jade/`.

4. Java CoG Kit. `http://www-unix.globus.org/cog/java/?CoGs=&`.

5. M. Atkinson. Structured Data and the Grid Access and Integration. http://www.nesc.ac.uk/talks/mpa/HPDC12Seattle23June03V2.pdf, June 2003.

6. R. Brandt and H. Reiser. Dynamic Adaptation of Mobile Agents in Heterogeneous Environments. In *proceedings of the 5th International Conference on Mobile Agents*, volume 2240, pages 70–87, 2001.

7. F. M. T. Brazier, B. J. Overeinder, M. van Steen, and N. J. E. Wijngaards. Agent Factory: Generative Migration of Mobile Agents in Heterogeneous Environments. In *proceedings of 2002 ACM Symposium on Applied Comp. (SAC 2002)*, pages 101–106), 2002.

8. Condor Project. `http://www.cs.wisc.edu/condor/`.

9. Condor Project. `http://www.cs.wisc.edu/condor/condorg/`.

10. R.P. Dick, D.L. Rhodes, and W. Wolf. TGFF: Task Graphs for Free. In *proceedings of International Workshop Hardware/Software Codesign*, pages 97–101, 1998.

11. Y. Feng and W. Cai. MCCF: A Distributed Grid Job Workflow Execution Framework. In *proceedings of the 2nd International Symposium on Parallel and Distributed Processing and Applications (ISPA'2004)*, pages 274–279, 2004.

12. Y. Feng and W. Cai. Execution Coordination in Mobile Agent based Distributed Job Workflow Execution. Technical report, Nanyang Technological University, 2007.

13. Y. Feng and W. Cai. Provenance Provisioning in Mobile Agent-Based Distributed Job Workflow Execution. In *proceedings of International Conference on Computational Science 2007 (ICCS 2007)*, pages 398–405. Part I, LNCS 4487, 2007.

14. Y. Feng, W. Cai, and J. Cao. Communication Partner Identification in Distributed Job Workflow Execution Over the Grid. In *proceedings of the 3rd International Workshop on Mobile Distributed Computing (in conjunction with the 25th IEEE International Conference on Distributed Computing Systems - ICDCS05)*, pages 587–593, 2005.

15. A. Fuggetta, G. P. Picco, and G. Vigna. Understanding Code Mobility. *IEEE Transactions on Software Engineering*, 24(5):342–361, 1998.

16. G. Heffelfinger and A. Geist. Report on the Computational Infrastructure Workshop for the Genomes to Life Program. `http://doegenomestolife.org/compbio/mtg\_1\_22\_02/infrastructure.pdf`, 2002.

17. A. Vahdat, K. Yocum, K. Walsh, P. Mahadevan, D. Kostic;, J. Chase, and D. Becker. Scalability and Accuracy in a Large-Scale Network Emulator. In *proceedings of the 5th symposium on Operating systems design and implementation (OSDI 02)*, pages 271–284, 2002.

18. J. Winick and S. Jamin. Inet-3.0: Internet topology generator. Technical Report CSE-TR-456-02, Computer Science Department, University of Michigan, Ann Arbor, MI, 2002.

19. J. Yan. *A Framework and Coordination Technologies for Peer-to-peer based Decentralised Workflow Systems*. PhD thesis, Swinburne University of Technology, 2004.

Grid Environment and Programming

RENDERING-ON-DEMAND SERVICE ACROSS HETEROGENEOUS GRID ENVIRONMENT

A/PROF. BU-SUNG LEE*, A/PROF. ALEXEI SOURIN*,
A/PROF. CLEMENT CHIA LIANG TIEN*, A/PROF. CHAN KAI YUAN*,
A/PROF. TERENCE HUNG†, QUOC-THUAN HO†, JIE WEI†,
DANNY OH‡, PROF. STEVEN MILLER‡,
ZHANG JUNWEI*, ANTHONY CHONG* and K. LEVINSKI*
CONTACT: EBSLEE@NTU.EDU.SG

*School of Computer Engineering, Nanyang Technological University
†A*STAR Institute of High-Performance Computing
‡School of Information Systems, Singapore Management University

Rendering of images is a very compute intensive task. Thus, it was chosen as one of the prospective commercial market that could leverage on grid/cluster technology. This paper reports on the development and deployment of grid rendering service across a heterogeneous grid environment. It covers the entire process from the submission of the jobs to management and rendering of the model. The prototype was successfully deployed and the results show the feasibility as well as the advantage of using the Grid in rendering animation.

1. Introduction

Over the years, we have seen the number of animation movies and the use of IT in enhancing/assisting in movie production. The use of IT has now become an integral part of the movie industry with IT companies working together with animation production companies [1, 2]. Figure 1 shows a generic workflow for the production of movie, or short animation clips.

As seen in Figure 1, the production of an animation sequence involves many tasks. One task that the IT industry is aggressively supporting is to provide the IT support for modeling and efficient rendering of image sequence. IT companies like HP has been aggressively engaging the movie industry in providing the rendering services. Take the example of the big animation movie that hit the scene is Shrek-2[1] which was a major, collaboration between Dreamwork and HP. HP has provided the HP Utility rendering technology on a cluster and the computational power of 1,000 CPUs to the rendering of the images.

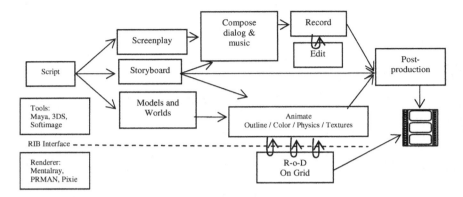

Figure 1: Simplified workflow of tasks involved in the development of animation movie.

Small and medium media production companies can ill afford to buy or tie-up with large IT companies. They would need an On-demand rendering service and charged based on its usage. Through our discussion with some companies, they indicated that they only have limited internal computation capability and their usage is bursty in nature. It is usually during the deadline that they need more resources. Thus, the goal of our project was to develop a Render-On-Demand (R-o-D) on Grid service to cater to the small and medium media production companies. On top of just helping with the current bursty demand, it will enable them to take on bigger production jobs without a higher IT outlay.

This paper is organized as follows. Section 2 will provide an overview of the system and provide a case study for the flow of a rendering task. Section 3 will describes in more detail the operation/design of the major modules in the system. Section 4 summarizes some of the major contribution of the project as well as some of its plans for the future.

2. R-o-D System Overview

Figure 2 shows the overview structure of the R-o-D system. User interacts with the R-o-D system via the portal. Jobs are submitted to the portal either through the web interface or via the Maya plug-in.

The portal will check for available resources on the Grid, by probing the Meta-schedulers. The system supports two different metaschedulers: Platform LSF Metaschdeuler [3] which is a commercial meta-scheduler and the IHPC metascheduler which is developed by the Institute of High Performance Computing [4]. The system and resource information obtained from the

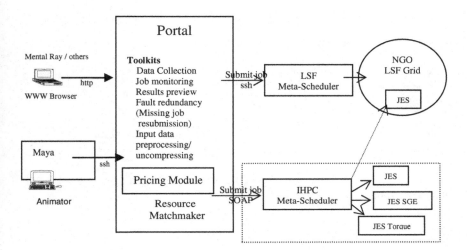

Figure 2: Components of Rendering on Demand (R-o-D) system.

metaschedulers are used by the Resource Matching Module to match with the user job requirements. Once the resources are identified, the portal will send the jobs to the respective clusters, via the metascheduler, for computation.

The portal will continuously monitor the status of the jobs, resubmitting lost jobs when detected. Once the job is completed the results are sent back to the portal, which will hold the rendered data in the respective user directory. The user can then preview the data and when satisfied with the results retrieve the data from the portal back into their system.

3. System Description

3.1. *Rendering Portal*

The portal is the single point of access to the R-o-D system. It provided a number of management modules. Figure 3 shows the different interfaces supported by the portal. The interface is crucial as the portal is a single point of access for the users.

The web interface is essential for user access to the Grid through the internet. Users can upload, monitor as well as download the rendered files. The image files are in the Renderman format (RIP). The portal is responsible for communicating with the metascheduler and forwarding the jobs to the previously selected servers via the metascheduler.

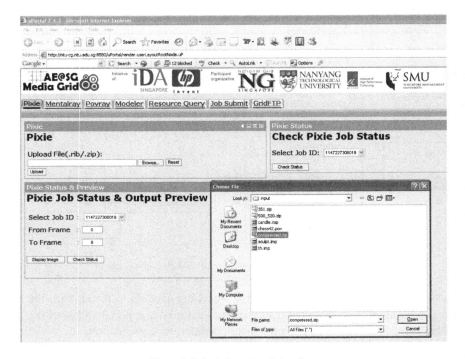

Figure 3: Submission via web interface.

The Maya plug-in was build so that Maya users can submit their rendering jobs to the Grid seamlessly within their application. The rendering models are also ftp across in Renderman format. However, it is noted that these RIP files are very large, as large as 700 Mbytes for a short 12 seconds animation. This is a major problem when the RIP files are transmitted across the commercial broadband network, as it would take a long time. To overcome this problem a special compression technique [13] was developed, which results in more than 100+ times reduction in file size.

3.2. *Information and Execution Management*

The ability of a grid to adapt effectively to the dynamic behavior of resources and activities is an important requirement. To be able to achieve this, up-to-date information on the entities and activities within the grid environment is needed – for doing resource matching, scheduling etc. The Information module functions to gather dynamic information about availability of resources, which cover software, which is provided to the resource-matching engine.

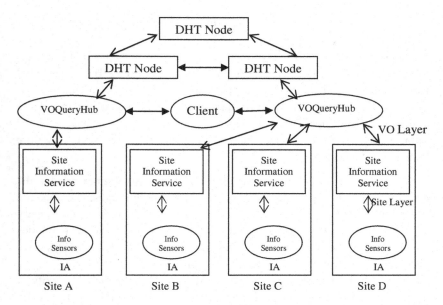

Figure 4: Overview of the Information module.

Our Information Service is a VO-oriented service with a hierarchical structure that comprises three layers: resource layer, site layer, and VO layer (as illustrated in Figure 4). This hierarchical framework matches the structure of a Grid Virtual Organization in a natural way, allowing more efficient management of information at different levels of the Grid infrastructure.

- The resource layer is the underlying layer of the Information Service. Physically it consists of all the resources being monitored in a Grid VO environment. The major components of the resource layer are the Information Sensor and Information Agent. Information Sensors are the basic mechanisms for capturing information about resources being monitored. They can be implemented in any programming language. Information Sensors are runtime hot-pluggable and dynamically integrated. An information agent (daemon) runs on each resource that is being monitored. It is responsible for invoking and monitoring the sensors to obtain up-to-date information on the monitored resources.

- Typically, there is a site-wide Information Service which is called the Site Information Service (SIS) running on an administrative domain site which participates in a Grid VO. By talking to the underlying Information Agents, an SIS aggregates information data from the resources being monitored in a domain. The SIS has caching mechanism to reduce query response time and improve throughput of queries.

- The VO layer federate SISs at different domain sites to present a global view of information in a large-scale Grid VO. We introduced a DHT (Distributed Hash Table) based peer-to-peer approach to create a virtual network of Site Information Services for information discovery and query in a large scale Grid VO. Under this P2P scheme, SISs collectively manage all the information in a Grid VO, without any fixed hierarchy, and with very little human assistance.

In addition, we proposed and implemented a security framework for the Information Service, which provides security policies for authentication and authorization control at both the site and the VO layers. To ease users to query the Information Service, we provide a set of SQL-style query interface that hides the complexity of Grid environments from the end users and provides easy access to resource information in a large scale Grid VO.

The Execution Management module was designed to hide the complexity of the Grid resources running at the back-end to do computational jobs. It provides a simple Distributed Resource Management Application API (DRMAA) [5] interface to access Grid resources. The developers can use DRMAA to submit jobs directly to the Job Execution Service (JES) that runs on top of a Grid resource. Here, the Grid resource can be a single computer or a cluster of computers with the local resource scheduler (e.g., Sun Grid Engine [6], Torque [7], or even LSF Metascheduler) running on the head node of the cluster. At this moment, we have demonstrated the ability to talk to LRMs such as Torque, SGE and LSF. The developers can also use DRMAA to submit jobs to different Grid resources through the metascheduler if the client cannot communicate directly with the Grid resources. In this scenario, the metascheduler acts as a bridge between the client and distributed Grid resources that are located in different domains. Detailed implementation and different execution models supported by the Execution Management module can be found in [4].

3.3. *Resource Matching*

Resource Matching is an important module that currently resides in the portal. The function of this module is to find the best matching resource that would meet the user requirements. The User can specify the resource definitions in high level manner, eg. CPU types, softwares, etc. In the development of this resource matching system, the formal representation of the resource types and the corresponding resource matchmaking system are studied.

The formal representation of the resource types is a prerequisite for the resource discovery. In our system we have adopted the Common Information Model(CIM)[8] as the Grid resource's domain knowledge's representation style. CIM provides a comprehensive model to specify concepts about a computing environment while remaining independent of platforms, protocols and implementations. The key advantage of CIM is its object oriented design pattern. According to our experiences in the Grid resource definition, we define the common resource types used in our portal system, whose hierarchical definition is shown in figure 5. Various resource types inherited from AE_LogicalResource are divided into software, operating system, CPU, memory, network interface, etc. Each of these resource types are further divided into specific resource types.

The matching of the resources is based on the semantic definition in Description Logic. Description Logics (DL)[9] is a well-known family of knowledge representation formalisms based on the notion of concepts (classes) and roles (properties). According to the similarity between the CIM and DL, we design the corresponding mapping algorithm. This mapping algorithm defines

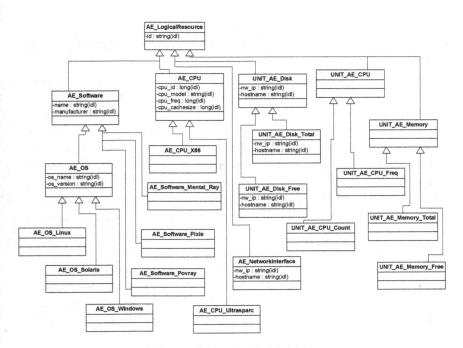

Figure 5: Common Information Model of Grid resource.

the rules to translate the CIM's classes, multiplicities, methods, associations, and inheritances to the correct DL constructs. By assigning formal DL semantics for the CIM, we are allowed to exploit formal results (e.g., w.r.t. the decidability and complexity of key inference problems) and algorithm designs from DL research, as well as to use DL based knowledge representation systems to provide reasoning support for matchmaking.

Matchmaking is defined as a process that requires a repository to take an inquiry as input, and to return all the published resource advertisements which are compatible with the resource requirements specified in the input inquiry. The match result is calculated as a level among *Exact, Subsume, Plugin, Intersection,* and *Disjoint.* The contexts with *Exact* and *Subsume* matching levels are returned back to the requester as satisfying results. *Exact* means the advertisement and the request are equivalent concepts, and *Subsume* means the request is sub-concept of the advertisement.

The implementation of the matching engine relies on the DL reasoning engine. The matching engine retrieves the resource information stored in CIM repository, converts it to the description logic, and matches it against the user's request by a DL reasoning engine. With the definition of match degrees, a DL reasoning engine can be used to match the request, such as Racer[10] and FaCT[11]. We use the Racer system to classify the taxonomy hierarchy for all resource advertisements. The classified taxonomy is used by Racer to increase the speed in the concepts' subsumption judgment. When the input inquiry concept R arrives, Racer is executed to judge the inquiry concept R's relationship with the advertisement concepts. Those with advertisement concepts equivalent to R are considered as *Exact* matches. Advertisement concepts that subsume but not equal to R are considered to be *Subsume* matches.

The matching engine's interface is wrapped as a Web Service to assist the integration with other system components. The interface contains two operations: the "match" method and the "update" method. The "match" method takes the user's resource inquiry as input and returns the matched resource. It has host level granularity currently. The "update" method invokes the information aggregator which pulls information from Information Service (IS) [12], aggregates it and then updates the CIM resource model in our repository. Figure 6 shows the way in which the matching engine integrates with the other system components. The matchmaker retrieves the sensor information from IS to update its repository. Portals query the matchmaker interface to get the matched resources.

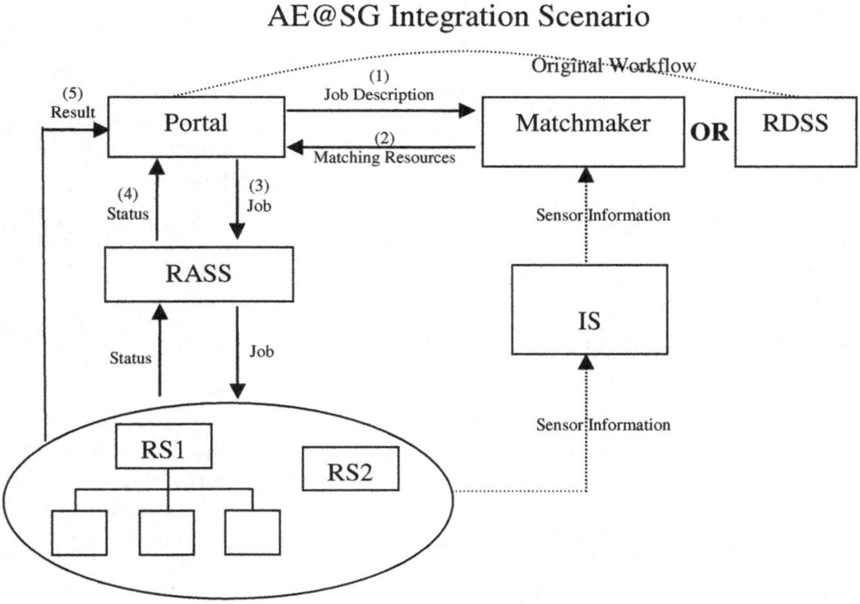

AE@SG Integration Scenario

Figure 6: Integration scenario.

The adoption of semantic web technology and CIM model has some unique advantages: the resources are formally defined in CIM as well as their hierarchical relationships to avoid any misunderstanding; matchmaking engine can take consideration of the relationships between the various resource types during the resource discovery; the resource definition in CIM repository can be extended easily to meet new resource types' appearance, and the system can map and match these new resource types without modification of the matching code base.

3.4. Pricing Module

The pricing module is responsible for capturing user resource usage and cost information. Two common market-driven pricing models are the posted pricing model and the auction-based pricing model. For the former model, resource owners publish pricing plans. Possible types of pricing plans include the following:

1) 3-part tariff

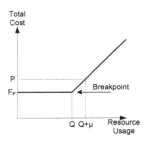

$$P = F_F + p*\mu$$

A user who accepts this tariff commits a fixed fee F_F for utilization level (or allowance) Q, and has an option to use additional units μ at a unit price p.

2) Special case 1: 2-part tariff

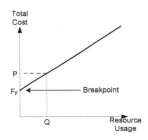

$$P = F_F + p*Q$$

A user who accepts this tariff pays a fixed access fee F_F and pays a variable fee to use units Q at a unit price p.

3) Special case 2: Linear tariff

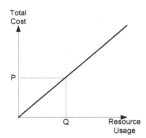

$$P = p*Q \ (F_F = 0)$$

A user who accepts this tariff pays a variable fee for Q units of utilization level at a unit price p.

4) Special case 3

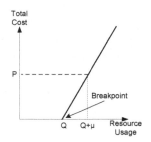

$$P = p*\mu \ (F_F = 0)$$

A user who accepts this tariff pays nothing for utilization level (or allowance) Q, and has an option to use additional units μ at a unit price p.

5) Special case 4

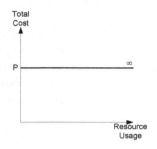

$$P = F_F$$

A customer who accepts this tariff pays a fixed fee F_F for unlimited utilization level.

6) Above pricing plans + guaranteed QoS

Pricing will be higher in these cases as resource providers will have to invest in server capacity to provide certain levels of QoS and these costs will be passed down to the users.

The auction-based pricing model was investigated using the HP Tycoon resource allocation system. Recent analysis [15] showed that the system might be difficult to use for normal users and it was difficult to provide service levels. On the other hand, it is easy for users to understand the posted pricing model which is based on the concept of pricing plans. For example, the mobile telecommunication industry has shown that end user would purchase the pricing plan that best suits his needs and service providers can adapt their service plans over time by learning from usage patterns. It was for this reason that we adopted the posted pricing model in our implementation. Users are required to purchase one out of the list of available pricing plans. Credit information (i.e. amount of available credits of current pricing plan) is highlighted whenever the user logs into the portal.

In brief, the pricing module consisted of two sub-modules:

1) Monitoring

This sub-module is responsible for capturing the resource usage information of the user. The Resource Usage Record format [14] is adopted and the information is stored in a MySQL database.

2) Billing

This sub-module is responsible for billing. The user is billed according to the current pricing plan and resource usage. Currently, only CPU time is used in the cost calculation. However, it should be noted that resources such as storage disk space and memory should be charged in the future.

4. Conclusion

The R-o-D system was last demonstrated to the public at GridAsia 2006. Rendering jobs were submitted to two clusters, 20 CPUs each, located at Institute of High Performance Computing and at Nanyang Technological University. A speed up of 17 times was achieved during the demonstration when 351 frames were rendered within 14 minutes. The less than linear speed up is due to the transfer time as well as the slight overhead due to the compression and decompression of the RIP files.

A number of technologies have been developed during the course of the project. Some of the major achievements are as follows;

- RIP file compression technology
- Resource matching engine using DL reasoning engine.
- Information and execution architecture.

The above technologies which were developed for the Animation industry are certainly applicable to other sectors of the industry, eg. finance, manufacturings. However, it is noted that each industry has its own peculiarities and customization would be necessary.

Acknowledgment

This project is supported by the Adaptive Enterprise @ Singapore Technology Alliance Scheme of the Infocomm Development Authority of Singapore.

References

1. "HP lab goes Hollywood", http: //www.hp.com/hpinfo/newsroom/feature_stories/2004/04hollywood.html.
2. SUN Microsystems Technology used in rendering Disney/PIXAR's "MONSTERS. INC" http://www.sun.com/smi/Press/sunflash/2001-11/sunflash.20011128.3.xml.
3. Platform LSF Metascheduler. http://www.platform.com.
4. Q.T. Ho, T. Hung, W. Jie, H.M. Chan, E. Sindhu, G. Subramaniam, T. Zang, and X. Li. GRASG - A Framework for "Gridifying" and Running Applications on Service-Oriented Grids. Proceedings of the 6th IEEE International Symposium on Cluster Computing and the Grid (CCGrid2006), Singapore, May 2006.
5. Distributed Resource Management Application API (DRMAA). http://www.drmaa.org.

6. Sun Grid Engine. http://gridengine.sunsource.net.
7. Torque Resource Manager. http://www.clusterresources.com/pages/products/torque-resource-manager.php.
8. D. M. T. F. Inc., "Common Information Model (CIM) Specification Version 2.2." available at: http://www.dmtf.org/standards/documents/CIM/DSP0004.pdf, 1999.
9. F. Baader, D. Calvanese, D. McGuinness, D. Nardi, and P. F. Patel-Schneider, *The Description Logic Handbook: Theory, Implementation, andApplications*: Cambridge University Press, 2003.
10. V. Haarslev, R. Moller, and M. Wessel, "RACER: Renamed ABox and Concept Expression Reasoner." available at: http://www.sts.tu-harburg.de/~r.f.moeller/racer.
11. P. Patel-Schneider and I. Horrocks, "DLP and FaCT," presented at TABLEAUX '99: Proceedings of the International Conference on Automated Reasoning with Analytic Tableaux and Related Methods, 1999.
12. W. Jie, T. Hung, and W. Cai, "An Information Service for Grid Virtual Organization: Architecture, Implementation and Evaluation," *The Journal of Supercomputing*, vol. 34, pp. 273-290, 2005.
13. A. Chong, A Sourin, K. Levinski, B.S. Lee, "A method and system for compressing and decompressing data" has been filed on 19 October 2006, ITTO Ref No.: PAT/036/06/06/SG.
14. H.K. Ng, Q.T. Ho, B.S. Lee, D. Lim, Y.S. Ong and W.T. Cai "Nanyang Campus Inter-Organisation Grid Monitoring System", Proceeding of Grid Computing and Application 2005.
15. D. Oh, S. Miller, "Economic Performance Analysis of the Tycoon Market-based Resource Allocation System for Grid Computing", In Proceedings of the 5th Workshop on e-Business, Milwaukee, WI, USA, Dec 9, 2006.

COLLABORATIVE WORKSPACE OVER
SERVICE-ORIENTED GRID

SHEN ZHIQI

Information Communication Institute of Singapore,
School of Electrical and Electronic Engineering,
Nanyang Technological University, 50 Nanyang Avenue, Singapore 637665

SHEN HAIFENG and MIAO CHUNYAN

School of Computer Engineering, Nanyang Technological University,
50 Nanyang Avenue, Singapore 637665

YANG ZHONGHUA, ROBERT GAY and ZHAO GUOPENG

Information Communication Institute of Singapore,
School of Electrical and Electronic Engineering,
Nanyang Technological University, 50 Nanyang Avenue, Singapore 637665

Grid computing has evolved dramatically, migrating to service oriented Grids: the third generation Grids. As a result, there has been great interest from both industry and the research community in enabling collaborative service provisioning through operational virtual communities over the grid. However, the existing service providing mechanism of the Grid is too rigid to provide the flexibility for a wide range of collaborative services. Lacking virtual community support at the operation level becomes a major barrier to promoting collaborative services over the Grid environment. In this paper we propose a collaborative workspace over service-oriented grid for developing operationally transparent virtual communities in a wide variety of domains.

1. Introduction

Grid is a type of parallel and distributed system that enables the sharing, selection, and aggregation of resources distributed across multiple administrative domains based on their (resources) availability, capability, performance, cost, and users' quality-of-service requirements [1]. Grid computing, since its emergence, has been an active research area for facilitating large-scale collaborative scientific research in many application domains such as geographic study, physical science, Genomics and etc. The initial focus is on the sharing of expensive resources, such as super computational power, storage and rare/expensive facilities. For example, the U.S. Network for Earthquake Engineering Simulation Grid (NEESGrid) connects experimental facilities (e.g., shake tables), data archives, and computers [2]. Nowadays grid computing has evolved dramatically, migrating to service oriented Grids: the third generation Grids [1, 3]. However, the existing Grid environment handles well how data and services are stored, represented and accessed, not the high level collaborative services in a virtual community. The existing service providing mechanism of the Grid is too rigid to provide the flexibility for a wide range of collaborative services. Lacking virtual community support at the operation level becomes a major barrier to promoting collaborative services over the Grid environment. As a result, there has been great interest from both industry and the research community in enabling collaborative service provisioning through operational virtual communities over the grid. For example, over the NEESGrid, a virtual community has been formed for information/knowledge sharing among earthquake scientists and engineers.

The advantages of having virtual communities on the grid are well known at the concept level, where like-minded individuals/groups share their knowledge/services for the benefit of all who participate, however, the practical implementation is still far from expectations. There have been recent efforts for exploration and deployment of domain specific virtual communities over the grid [4, 5]. However, the lack of a common and widely accepted methodology as well as supporting framework is still forcing every vertical development project to design and implement its own home-grown mini virtual community framework in a specific application domain.

Collaborative services provision needs the real collaboration in operation level in a collaborative workspace of virtual community environment. Without efficient support from dynamic virtual community formation mechanisms, transparent virtual community operation tools, virtual community support services, virtual community management services etc., collaborative services cannot be effectively composed. In order to leverage the potential benefits of virtual community paradigm, there is a great need for proposing practical methodology and developing flexible and generic framework to support the formation, and operation of virtual community in various application domains. To date, little work has been reported on Operationally Transparent Virtual Communities that supports collaborative workspaces over the Grid.

In this research we propose and design and implement a collaborative workspace for developing operationally transparent virtual communities in a wide variety of domains such as manufacturing grid, bioinformatics grid, digital media grid, and various collaborative e-research, e-science and e-services grid.

This research aims to provide a systematic solution to Operationally Transparent Virtual Communities over the service-oriented Grid in a wide range of application domains and attempts to meet the challenges we faced.

Following this introduction, Section 2 describes the architecture of our proposed collaborative workspace. Section 3 presents the implementation of the community portal built on top of the collaborative workspace. Users can work collaboratively using the proposed workspace through this portal. Finally the paper is concluded in Section 4.

2. Collaborative Workspace

The Virtual grid community is based on a service-oriented grid infrastructure. The collaborative workspace supporting the virtual communities is composed of six components, as shown in Figure 1, which are virtual community (VC) management, transparent collaborative tools for virtual community operation, process management for automating the collaborative processes, virtual community supporting services, knowledge management and trust management in virtual community.

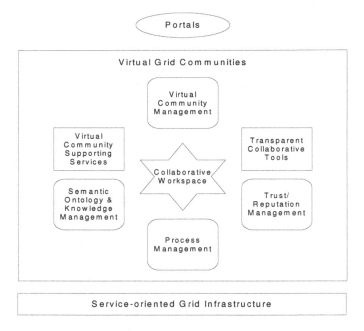

Figure 1. A Reference Model for Operational Transparent Virtual Community over Service-oriented Grid.

The component transparent collaborative tools for virtual community operation, process management for automating the collaborative processes, and trust management in virtual community provides sophisticated framework and transparent collaborative tools for collaborations in an operation level for the need of meaningful collaboration between VC members across organizations, locations etc. in the collaborative workspace over grid environment.

2.1. *Goal Oriented Process Modeling and Scheduling*

One important aspect in the VC is to model and schedule the processes in the collaborative workspace. The activities carried out by a company are usually organized in groups of inter-related activities called processes that can be seen as a set of activities, rules and constraints specifying the steps that must be taken, and conditions that must be satisfied, in order to accomplish a given goal. In this research, we adopt goal-oriented approach, Goal Net [6], for process modeling and scheduling. The advantages to use Goal Net include:

- Goal Net is a novel goal oriented process modeling tool which can decompose a complex process to executable sub-processes for achieving a common goal.
- Goal Net is a multi-agent modeling tool by which a multi-agent system can be derived from the process modeling for automating the processes.

With Goal Net, the composition of each process is designed in order to achieve a specific goal. A business process can be decomposed into a hierarchy of sub processes and activities. Parts of the decomposition of this process are assigned to different organizations or VC members. A combination of various processes takes place at different members in order to achieve the global goal of the high level process. The problem of the supervision or coordination of such a process at its various levels of decomposition is critical, in this context, where its definition and activity are not limited to a single organization, but to a set of autonomous, distributed, and heterogeneous nodes that need to cooperate. With Goal Net, the supervision and coordination are automatically derived during the process decomposition phase.

The development framework and tool, MADE (multi-agent development environment) [7] is used and extended to web platform in our research for business process modeling, agent creation, service scheduling and execution of distributed processes that dynamically compose/integrate the services provided by different community members. UDDI [8] from web service community is used for service specification/definition and service registration.

2.2. *Collaboration Workspace and Transparent Collaborative Tools*

To enable operational transparent virtual community, it is required to integrate multiple participates into a coherent, structured, and collaborative management process. Such a collaborative management process can be built on the basis of the shared collaborative workspace, where team members exchange their updates on the shared artifact and maintain a consistent state of it.

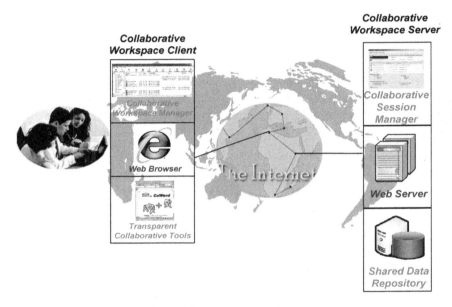

Figure 2. A Collaborative Workspace.

As shown in Figure 2, a collaborative workspace consists of a server component and a client component. The server component provides a data repository for storing artifacts to be shared by a virtual community and a collaborative session manager that coordinates collaborative users, e.g., joining into and quitting from a collaborative session and exchange of updates made on shared artifacts. Accordingly, the client component has a collaborative workspace manager [9] for viewing and manipulating the shared data repository, such as creating, deleting folders and files and changing their access rights; for viewing collaborative session information, such as what are available sessions, who are the participants in each session; and for starting a new session or joining an existing session by launching a collaborative tool.

To take advantage of Web's ubiquitous accessibility and file sharing capability over the Grid, the collaborative workspace is built upon the Web platform. In particular, the server component extends an existing web server to support collaborative session management and shared data repository management. The client component has been specially designed to manipulate the shared data repository, and to start a new session or join an existing collaborative session by launching a collaborative tool. As file management of web folders are often integrated in web browsers such as Internet Explorer (IE), our approach extends a web browser to support collaborative workspace management. This approach is called Transparent Adaptation (TA) [10, 12], which extends an off-the-shelf single-user application for collaborative use without modifying the original application, thus being transparent.

Figure 3. The Transparent Adaptation Approach.

The TA approach provides a bridge between state-of-the-art collaborative technologies and off-the-shelf mainstream single-user applications. As shown in Figure 3, the TA approach consists of three major components. The top component is the Single-user Application (SA), which provides conventional functionalities. The SA can be any existing or new applications such as Web browsers, Office applications, and Integrated Programming Environments. The base component is Generic Collaborative Engine (GCE), which provides advanced collaborative capabilities. The GCE component can be reused in adapting different single-user applications. The middle component Collaboration Adaptor (CA) bridges the gap between the SA and the GCE components.

Collaborative tools that have been investigated or are under investigation in this research include collaborative web browsers, collaborative office applications [11, 12], and collaborative integrated programming environments.

2.3. *Trust Management*

In the collaborative workspace environment, services from virtual organizations are shared and cooperate among all the members. Security and trust is an important issue for the successful collaborations. Traditional security analysis cannot sufficiently protect each sub-service atomically. The manufacturing grid environment provides an open, decentralized infrastructure that spans multiple administrative domains. Trust Management (TM) is an emerging framework for decentralizing security decisions that helps users in asking "why" trust is granted rather than immediately focusing on "how" cryptography can enforce it. In this research, we propose and implement a pragmatic method for Trust Modeling and Management in virtual grid community [13]. TM is integrated into the collaborative workspace for document authoring and distribution, content filtering, and service provision/selection.

3. Community Portal

In the last section, the major components of the transparent workspace are presented. To allow VC members to work collaboratively in this workspace, we design and implement a community portal on the Web. With this portal, VC members can share their services to other members and use available services for their own business needs without knowing where the services are located. In the following sub-sections, the system architecture is introduced first. Then, the system design and implementation are described. Finally, the application areas of this research are discussed.

3.1. *Collaborative Workspace Architecture*

The system is designed in a layered structure.

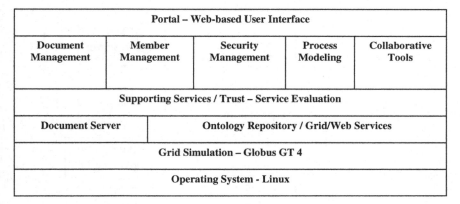

Figure 4. The Collaborative Workspace Architecture.

As shown in Figure 4, the lowest layer is the operating system running on different grids. Then it is the GT4 [14] layer which provides grid services. Layer 3 is the service layer containing the Grid services, web services, and content services, etc. Layer 4 provides the trust evaluation service at which all the grid/web services will be evaluated. During the business process execution, the grid/web service will be selected dynamically through the trust service. Layer 5 is the interface support tools including content management, community member management, security management, process modeling tool, and the collaborative tools. Finally Layer 6 is the portal layer at which users can access the collaborative workspace through the community portal.

3.2. Implementation

As shown in Figure 5, the system contains the following components:

- Application server that supports web server, java servlet container, and web service adaptor;
- UDDI server that provides UDDI registry services;
- Database server that stores the data;
- Transparent tool engine that provides the transparent collaborative work environment;
- Trust service engine that provides the trust service;
- MADE framework that provides business process modeling, agent creation and agent execution services; and
- Other tools that provides other services including content managements, member management, chatting, and forum, etc.

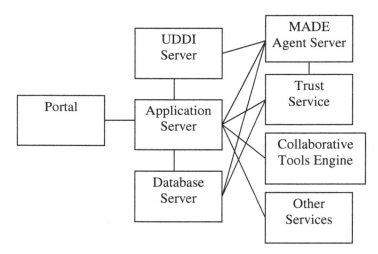

Figure 5. The Portal System Structure.

As shown in the screen shot in Figure 6, the portal provides many services for users to join the community and do the collaborative work with other community members. For examples, users can share documents by clicking the resource button, chat with other members by joining a chatting room, join the forum to discuss with other members by entering a forum group.

To work with the collaborative workspace, users can join the community as service providers or service consumers. When a user provides a service, he can register the service through the service registration page by clicking the service button. Then the service will be automatically registered into the community UDDI server. To consume the service, users can design a business process using the process modeling tool by clicking the process button. When you define a process in the modeling tool, the available services in the UDDI server and functions will be shown in the service panel and function panel respectively. Users can model the business process by drag and drop the selected service or function into the process modeling panel. When the process is executed, the agent will invoke the services according to the process model. The services will be evaluated timely by the trust service when they are used. When there is more than one the same service available in the protal, the trust service will be used to select the service.

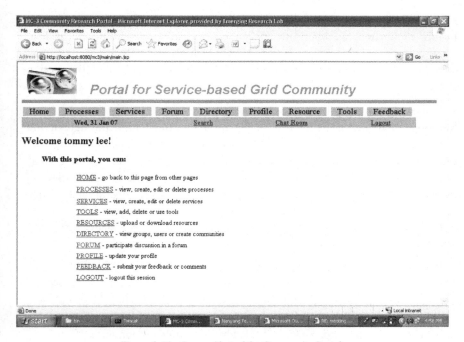

Figure 6. The Screen Shot of the Community Portal.

3.3. *Applications*

Grid enables sharing, selection and aggregation of resources distributed across multiple administrative domains. However, the success of the Grid requires effective community mechanisms to realize collaboration among the collaborators. The transparent collaborative workspace and operational virtual community environment developed in this research can be applied to many application domains. In this section, we outline a few potential applications and areas that can be exploited:

• Virtual Community for Integrated Manufacturing Grid Services
Currently, most organizations/enterprises are connected to the Internet. With manufacturing Grid, the service-oriented view of resources of supply chains as services enables on demand services. Users are able to select services for their business objectives without being aware of the suppliers and locations. Operational Virtual community and transparent collaborative workspace provide users a single place to collaborate with others for composing new services.

- Virtual Community for CAD/CAM Collaborative Design

In this application, we intend to apply the transparent adaptation approach to some commercial systems such as CAD/CAM tools, Knowledge Management tools, and Web browsers so that users are able to conduct collaborative design through these tools in a virtual community.

- Virtual Community for Life Science Product Design

Recently, there has been interest in the need to extend high throughput life science research to bio-manufacturing. This initiative in bio-manufacturing is to connected the current broad base of life science research to manufacturing areas and translate the technological know-how and research output into designs and manufactured products. In this application, we provide operational virtual community mechanisms to manage participants and grid services for life science, and provide collaborative workspace for users to share resources, schedule services and make collaboration plans, etc.

- Virtual Community for Collaborative e-Research

The virtual communities allow their members to share research resources and grid services, and interact with one another for both collaborative work and social purposes. Members at different offices and those working from home can share a mutual sense of presence provided by the virtual community.

- Virtual Community for e-Learning

A virtual learning community enables learners to interact in a common online environment to gain understanding of subject matter. Learners can select and assemble learning objects provided by different learning grids and obtain personalized learning paths. They can share a common learning goal and interact socially through the community.

4. Conclusions

In this paper, an operational transparent virtual community environment that supports collaborative workspace is proposed and developed to provide a common platform to enable collaborative service provision in a grid environment. Compared to other Grid community portals, the presented transparent workspace has the following advantages:

- VC members can provide and consume services in single place in the consistent manner without knowing where the services are located;
- VC members can use the goal oriented process modeling tool to model their business processes using the available services and functions provided in the

community through the portal; and to execute the process through the same portal;

- VC members can work on the same design work or the same documents collaboratively, and simultaneously at different locations using the transparent tools; and
- Trust service can evaluate the services that are used by consumers so that it can provide recommendations to the service selection when the same services are available.

We have also discussed the potential applications of our research. In our ongoing project, we are building communities in bioinformatics and e-learning domains respectively using the proposed collaborative workspace. The research results, including system architecture, development framework, prototype system, research documents are not tied to a specific domain. They can be transferred to a wider range of application domains including manufacturing, digital media, engineering, life science, chemistry, physics etc.

Acknowledgement

This research is partially supported by the project sponsored by the National Grid Office/A*STAR of Singapore (Grant number is 052 015 0024).

References

1. R. Buyya, D. Abramson and J. Giddy, "A case for economy grid architecture for service oriented grid computing", *Proceedings of the 15th International Symposium on Parallel and Distributed Processing.*, pp. 776–790, 23-27 April, 2001.
2. NeesGrid Home Page, http://www.neesgrid.org/.
3. I. Foster, C. Kesselman, J. Nick and S. Tuecke, "The Physiology of the Grid: An Open Grid Services Architecture for Distributed Systems Integration", *Open Grid Service Infrastructure WG, Global Grid Forum*, June 22, 2002.
4. Z. G. Hai, "Clustering soft-devices in the semantic grid", *Computing in Science & Engineering*, Volume 4, Issue 6, pp. 60–62, 2002.
5. G. Boella, L. van der Torre, "Local policies for the control of virtual communities", *Proceedings of IEEE/WIC International Conference on Web Intelligence (WI 2003)*, pp. 161–167, 13-17 Oct. 2003.
6. Z. Q. Shen, C. Y. Miao and R. Gay, "Goal Oriented Modeling for Intelligent Software Agents", *Proceedings of the 2004 IEEE/WIC/ACM*

International Conference on Intelligent Agent Technology (IAT'04), Beijing, China, September 20 - 24, 2004.

7. Z. Q. Shen, C. Y. Miao and R. Gay, "Goal-oriented Methodology for Agent-oriented Software Engineering", *IEICE Transactions on Information and Systems, Special Issue on Knowledge-based Software Engineering*, Vol. E89-D, No. 4, April, 2006.

8. UDDI: Universal Description, Discover and Integration of Business for the Web, http://www.uddi.org.

9. H. Shen, S.P. Zhou, C. Sun and Z.W. Phyo, "A Generic WebDAV-based Document Repository Manager for Collaborative Systems," *The 2006 IEEE/WIC/ACM Conference on Web Intelligence (WI'06)*, pp. 129-136, Hong Kong, December 18-22, 2006.

10. H. Shen and C. Sun, "Leveraging Single-User Applications for Multiuser Distributed Collaboration," *IEEE Distributed Systems Online*, vol. 7, no. 4, pp 15-21, art. no. 0406-04002, April 2006.

11. H. Shen and S. Zhou, "Reconciliation of Compound Actions in Internet-based Distributed Collaborative Systems", *International Journal of High Performance Computing Networks*, accepted to appear in 2007.

12. C. Sun, S. Xia, D. Sun, D. Chen, H. Shen and W. Cai, "Transparent adaptation of single-user applications for multi-user real-time collaboration", ACM Transactions on Computer Human Interaction. Vol. 13, No. 4, pp. 1-52, December, 2006.

13. J. S. Weng, C. Y. Miao, A. Goh, Z. Q. Shen and R. Gay, "Trust-based Agent Community for Collaborative Recommendation", *the Fifth International Joint Conference on Autonomous Agents and Multiagent Systems (AAMAS 2006)*, Future University, Hakodate, Japan, 8 - 12 May, 2006.

14. Globus toolkit, http://www.globus.org/.

OPAL OP: AN EXTENSIBLE GRID-ENABLING WRAPPING TOOL FOR LEGACY APPLICATIONS

K. ICHIKAWA and S. DATE

Osaka Research Center, NICT
Osaka University,
1-1, Yamadaoka, Suita, Osaka 565-0871, Japan
E-mail: {ichikawa, date}@ais.cmc.osaka-u.ac.jp

S. KRISHNAN and W. LI

University of California San Diego,
9500 Gilman Dr., La Jolla, CA 92093, USA
E-mail: {sriram, wilfred}@sdsc.edu

K. NAKATA, Y. YONEZAWA, H. NAKAMURA and S. SHIMOJO

Osaka University,
E-mail: nakata@chem.sci.osaka-u.ac.jp,
{yasuyon3, harukin}@protein.osaka-u.ac.jp, shimojo@cmc.osaka-u.ac.jp

This paper describes a new approach (Opal OP: Opal Operation Provider) to wrap existing legacy applications as Grid services. In order to expose, with minimal effort, existing applications as Grid services, Opal OP provides a method for wrapping a legacy application as a program module, or as an operation provider. Traditional wrapping methods usually restrict the way to implement Grid services because these methods provide only a suite of interfaces necessary for using the wrapped application. The proposed Opal OP, on the other hand, doesn't restrict the way to implement a Grid service from a legacy application. Opal OP is implemented as an operation provider that wraps the application and thus can be used as a module in the Grid service. Application developers can easily develop their own services where legacy applications are wrapped through the utilization of Opal OP. In this paper, we show some scientific applications including a bio-molecular simulation system developed as Grid services using Opal OP. The results show the usefulness and effectiveness of Opal OP.

1. Introduction

Various scientific simulation programs have been emerging with the advance of computational simulation technologies. There has been a tendency for scientists and researchers to integrate such simulation programs into a single more advanced simulation program in a multi-scale and multi-physics manner[1]. This current trend is explained by the scientists and researchers' desire to understand their target phenomena more accurately.

Recent performance improvement in computing and networking technologies has led to the advancement of distributed computing typified by Grid computing. The latest Grid middleware represented by the OGSA and WSRF standards aim to integrate services-oriented architecture (SOA) into Grid computing[2]. In this concept, programs are supposed to be implemented as services and interoperate with each other via service interfaces. In this context, the services represent Web services or Grid services, which are instantiated through Grid middleware.

Despite the maturity of Grid middleware, the methods for exposing existing applications as services have not been well developed. Wrapping methods that execute a command line application and then provide interfaces to access the result of the execution have been studied as one possible way to easily expose applications as services. Such wrapping methods provide only the generic interfaces necessary for using the wrapped application, such as job submission, and job monitoring. These generic interfaces are designed and implemented by the developers of these wrapping tools for application developers. In reality, however, there is little flexibility or extensibility in development. For example, application developers cannot implement application specific interfaces in the Grid service realized by such traditional wrapping methods.

In this paper, we show a wrapping tool, Opal Operation Provider (Opal OP), which allows application developers to easily build a Grid service from a legacy application. How the problem of inflexibility and inextensibility is solved in our tool is shown. Section 2 clarifies the focus of our research by overviewing previous efforts related to wrapping methods. Section 3 describes the architecture of Opal OP. Section 4 shows some examples including our bio-molecular simulation system using the Opal OP. Section 5 concludes this paper.

2. Related Works and Our Focus

Until recently, several wrapping methods, which allow application developers to easily build a Grid service from a legacy application, have been proposed and implemented. The following are typical examples.

- Opal[3]: provides a wrapping service based on Web services.

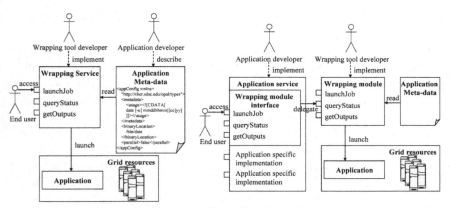

Figure 2.   Extensible wrapping service model

Figure 1.   Wrapping service model

- GEMLCA[4]: provides a wrapping service based on GT3.
- GAP service[5]: provides a wrapping service based on In-VIGO framework developed at the University of Florida.
- Gfac[6]: provides a wrapping service based on XSOAP/XSUL developed at Indiana University.

All of these methods focus on wrapping a command line based application as a Grid or Web service and providing generic interfaces for launching the application on Grid resources and then accessing the results after the application execution. These methods have a common architecture based on the wrapping service model shown in Figure 1. In this model, there are three actors: An application developer, a wrapping tool developer and an end user. To wrap applications automatically, the wrapping service offered by these wrapping methods requires meta-data described by the application developers. The meta-data contains the description necessary for executing the application, such as where the binary of the application is located, and how to launch the application. In response to requests from end users, the service submits jobs into Grid resources by using the meta-data.

Although this wrapping model is helpful to application developers who just want to convert their own application to a Grid service, this wrapping model cannot satisfy the requirements of the application developers who want to extend and further develop the Grid service wrapping their own applications. The reason is explained from the fact that these wrapping methods, except for Gfac, never assume the application developers' extension, and thus, provide only a limited suite of interfaces for using the wrapping service.

Unlike other wrapping methods, Gfac has a mechanism to extend generic interfaces of services. The mechanism ensures extensibility in development by adding a pre-process and a post-process routine into the services dynamically. However, this doesn't mean that the mechanism enables application developers to design their services freely.

Our research is differentiated from these wrapping methods in terms of the research focus. We aim to provide development flexibility to application developers who want to further develop and extend the Grid service wrapping their legacy applications. Figure 2 indicates our wrapping service model adopted in this research. The difference from the model shown in Figure 1 is that legacy applications are wrapped as a program module, which can be usable from the Grid service. This model's advantage is that the implementation of wrapping modules and application specific implementation are separated. Thus, wrapping tool developers can concentrate on the design and implementation of wrapping features, whereas application developers concentrate on solving application specific problems.

3. Opal Operation Provider (Opal OP)

We have adopted Opal as a building block technology to realize the extensible service model shown in Figure 2. Opal is developed by the National Biomedical Computation Resource (NBCR) at the University of California San Diego (UCSD). Specifically, Opal has been utilized to provide the wrapping functionality of legacy programs through the standard technology of Grid services and Web services. Also, Opal is designed to be simple for wrapping command line applications. It doesn't have any unnecessary features other than those for wrapping applications. This is the reason that Opal can be suitably integrated as a wrapping operation provider. In this section, we explain the concept of operation provider, and then introduce the design and implementation of the proposed Opal OP.

3.1. *Operation Provider*

The operation provider is a basic implementation technology used in Globus Toolkit 4 (GT4). The primary features of GT4 such as WS-Resource Framework (WSRF) and WS-Notification (WSN) standards are realized by operation providers. As the name indicates, the operation provider offers a way to provide the operations defined in it to other Grid services. In this

Figure 3. sample_service.wsdl

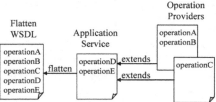

Figure 4. Flatten process

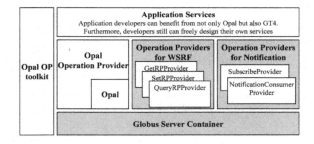

Figure 5. The software hierarchy of Opal OP in GT4 architecture

context, operations mean operations defined in the WSDL. By using an operation provider, a service can import operations defined in the operation provider without modifying the implementation of the service.

In order to use operation providers, application developers have to describe the names of operation providers in an "extends" attribute in the WSDL of their application as shown in Figure 3. In this way, the service can import definitions of operations from operation providers. The build tool shipped with GT4 gathers all interfaces specified in the "extends" attribute in the WSDL, and then generates a large WSDL file containing all operations. This task is called "flatten" as shown in Figure 4. End users can access all operations via this flatten WSDL file. If end users call an operation in a service implemented by an application developer, GT4 container dispatches the request to the service. On the other hand, if end users call an operation provided by an operation provider, the container dispatches the request to the operation provider. This model is similar to the delegation model in object-oriented architecture.

3.2. *Opal OP and Opal OP Toolkit*

Figure 5 shows the software hierarchy of Opal OP in GT4 architecture. The Opal OP and Opal OP toolkit were developed in our research. The gray boxes show software components implemented in GT4. Opal OP implements wrapping features as one of the operation providers in GT4, so that application developers can use the wrapping features in the same manner as other operation providers of GT4. Application developers can adopt the wrapping features of Opal OP into their application services easily. Furthermore, they can still extend and implement their services where their applications are wrapped by Opal OP.

The Opal OP toolkit supports the development and use of services using Opal OP. Opal OP has the advantage over the existing wrapping methods in ensuring flexibility in development. However, to utilize the operation provider, application developers have to write codes to implement services and configure WSDL as shown in the previous section. The Opal OP toolkit is developed to minimize this task and provide usability equivalent to traditional wrapping methods. The Opal OP toolkit supports the following two tasks.

First, the Opal OP toolkit supports the development, building, and deployment of a service using Opal OP. The Opal OP toolkit generates template codes and configuration files for the service, so that application developers do not need to write any codes to use Opal OP. Also, the Opal OP toolkit automates the process from building to deployment of the service into a GT4 container. In this way, the application developers' tasks are minimized to the equivalent tasks in traditional wrapping methods.

Second, the Opal OP toolkit provides command-line tools to access services using Opal OP. End users need to use WSRF based SOAP API and write codes to access the wrapping services. Every wrapping service extends the interface from Opal OP. Therefore, all of these services can be accessed in the same manner. The Opal OP toolkit provides generic command-line tools using this common interface to submit a job and to query a job status. Thus, even if end users are not familiar with Web services technologies, they can use the wrapping services by these command-line tools.

In order to develop a service which wraps an application using Opal OP and the Opal OP toolkit, application developers just need to do the following tasks: (1) Create a properties file describing the information used for the code generation of the service, (2) Launch a toolkit command to create a service, (3) Launch a toolkit command to build and deploy the service

```
interface.name=Date
binary.location=/bin/date
target.namespace=http://biogrid.jp/namespaces/DateService
package=jp.biogrid.services.date
stubs.package=jp.biogrid.stubs.date
prefix.publish.path=example/date
factory.target.namespace=http://biogrid.jp/namespaces/DateFactoryService
```

Figure 6.   DateService.properties

into GT4. Figure 6 shows an example of properties file. In the process of creating a service, codes of wrapping service and configuration files of Opal are generated by using this properties file. These tasks to develop services which wrap applications are very simple. Application developers can create services which wrap existing applications without having to write any codes. If application developers need to extend the implementation of the service, they can modify the generated source codes freely. Also, operation providers are the basis of GT4 implementation technologies, and the services using Opal OP have a high affinity with GT4 technologies.

4. Examples of Applications Using Opal OP

We have been developing several simulation services using Opal OP. In this section, we introduce a bio-molecular simulation system as an example of Grid applications using Opal OP. Also, we show a protein structure similarity search system and a drug docking simulation system as examples of easy service development.

4.1. *QM/MM Hybrid Simulation System*

We have been developing a QM/MM hybrid simulation system to simulate bio-molecular behaviors. This system calculates forces interacting among atoms at short time steps (e.g. 0.5 fsec), and then simulates molecular behavior by repeating these calculations tens of thousands of times. Our QM/MM hybrid simulation system consists of two applications. One is AMOSS[7] based on Quantum Mechanics (QM), and the other is cosgene[8] based on Molecular Dynamics Mechanics (MM). The QM-based calculation is time-consuming, but has high accuracy. The MM based calculation is fast, but has low accuracy. We have been trying to develop a highly accurate and large scale bio-molecular simulation by adopting QM-based calculations

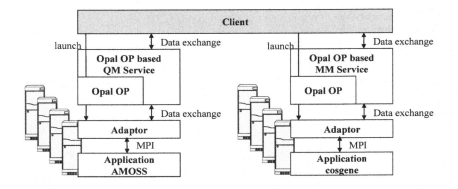

Figure 7.   The overview of the QM/MM hybrid simulation system

to the important part of the simulation and MM based calculations to the remaining parts.

In order to calculate molecular behavior, these two applications have to exchange data at every time step while the two applications are running. This kind of requirement in computation cannot be handled by the traditional wrapping approaches. To handle this kind of requirement, a mechanism like Opal OP is needed that can handle application specific problems. We have implemented a QM/MM hybrid simulation system using the following three steps. Figure 7 shows an overview of the architecture of the system implemented by the Opal OP.

First, in order to hide complexity of the dynamic process creation of QM and MM programs from a local scheduler and then enable the synchronization between the two programs, we have developed adapter programs. Both QM and MM programs consist of several program modules, and the modules are executed and combined by a dynamic process creation method (spwan) of MPI-2. The adapter programs hide such dynamic process creation and make the applications simple MPI programs. Also, these adapter programs help to synchronize QM and MM programs to exchange data using a traditional file lock mechanism. When calculations of each simulation step start, the adapter creates a lock file, and then removes it after the step is over. By checking the existence of the lock file, the timing for transferring data is known.

Second, we wrapped the adapter programs by Opal OP. For this process, we did not need to write any codes. We configured these services as parallel applications in the Opal's application meta-data file.

Finally, we added operations to exchange data into the services generated by Opal OP. Also, we added operations to check the lock files for synchronization. For this task, we do not need to consider how the Opal OP wrapped the application.

Generally, application developers find it difficult to develop this kind of service from scratch. Using Opal OP, we concentrated only on how to synchronize two applications in the process of development. This is the advantage brought about by Opal OP.

4.2. Protein Structure Similarity-Search System and Drug-Docking Simulation System

In this section, we describe a protein structure similarity search system and a drug-docking simulation system.

The protein structure similarity-search system[9] is developed as a Web portal with Java servlet technologies, and uses a protein structure similarity searching program as a backend program. To distribute the processes of the backend program, the system needs to use Grid technologies. A developer, who is not familiar with Grid technologies, has developed protein structure similarity-search services using Opal OP, and has developed a Web portal which accesses the services via the interfaces with SOAP. The developer had no knowledge of Grid technologies, but it took only several weeks to build such a system, with most of the time focused on application specific requirements, instead of Grid service development.

The drug-docking simulation system has been developed by a UCSD undergraduate student whose major is bio-engineering. The system uses DOCK, a docking program for drug discovery. To benefit from a large amount of computational resources, Opal OP-based docking services, which wrap DOCK, were developed and deployed into Grid resources. Although the student was not familiar with computer science or Grid technologies, he was able to use the generic command-line tools provided in the Opal OP toolkit to access the services. He used with ease the command-line tools in shell scripting to build the distributed drug docking simulation system. It took only several weeks to build this system, with most of the time spent learning Perl programming.

These examples show how the development of services is made simple by using Opal OP in comparison with the development of service using traditional wrapping methods. This approach enables the building of services that wrap existing applications without knowledge of Grid technologies.

5. Conclusions

This paper described a new method to build wrapping services using Opal OP. Opal OP was implemented as an operation provider of GT4, allowing application developers to easily build a Grid service. By separating the implementation of the wrapping features and application services, the Opal OP provides a flexible way to build wrapping services.

We also showed a bio-molecular simulation system as an example of an application that takes advantage of Opal OP. Through this example, we explained that Opal OP did not affect the implementation of the application services, and thus application developers could concentrate on solving application specific problem. The examples of a protein structure similarity-search system and a drug-docking simulation system were shown to explain how the development of services was made simple through the use of Opal OP.

References

1. Haruki Nakamura, Susumu Date, Hideo Matsuda, and Shinji Shimojo. A challenge towards next-generation research infrastructure for advanced life science. *New Generation Computing*, 22(2), February 2004.
2. I. Foster, C. Kesselman, J. Nick, and S. Tuecke. The physiology of the grid: An open grid services architecture for distributed systems integration. In *Open Grid Service Infrastructure WG*. Global Grid Forum, June 2002.
3. Sriram Krishnan, Brent Stearn, Karan Bhatia, Kim K. Baldridge, Wilfred Li, and Peter Arzberger. Opal: Simple web services wrappers for scientific applications. In *IEEE International Conference on Web Services (ICWS'06)*, pages 823–832, September 2006.
4. Peter Kacsuk, Tamas Kiss, Ariel Goyeneche, Thierry Delaitre, Zoltan Farkas, and Tamas Boczko. High-level grid application environment to use legacy codes as ogsa grid services. In *5th IEEE/ACM International Workshop on Grid Computing*, pages 428– 435, November 2004.
5. Vivekananthan Sanjeepan, Andrea M. Matsunaga, Liping Zhu, Herman Lam, and Jose A. B. Fortes. A service-oriented, scalable approach to grid-enabling of legacy scientific applications. In *The 2005 IEEE International Conference on Web Services (ICWS 2005)*, pages 553–560, July 2005.
6. Gopi Kandaswamy, Liang Fang, Yi Huang, Satoshi Shirasuna, Suresh Marru, and Dennis Gannon. Building web services for scientific grid applications. *IBM Journal of Research and Development*, 50(2/3):249–260, 2006.
7. Toshihiro Sakuma, Hiroshi Kashiwagi, Toshikazu Takada, and Haruki Nakamura. Ab initio MO study of the chlorophyll dimer in the photosynthetic reaction center. i. a theoretical treatment of the electrostatic field created by the surrounding proteins. *Int. J. Quant. Chem.*, 61:137–151, 1997.

8. Yoshifumi Fukunishi, Yoshiaki Mikami, and Haruki Nakamura. The filling potential method: A method for estimating the free energy surface for protein-ligand docking. *J. Phys. Chem. B.*, 107:13201–13210, 2003.

9. Reiko Yamashita, Daron M. Standley, Kohei Ichikawa, and Haruki Nakamura. Grid web service using opal operation provider. In *The 3rd International Life Science Grid Workshop (LSGRID2006)*, October 2006.

SECURITY MONITORING EXTENSION FOR MOGAS

S. TAKEDA and S. DATE

Osaka Research Center,
National Institute of Information and Communications Technology
and
Graduate School of Information Science and Technology,
Osaka University, Japan
5-1 Mihogaoka, Ibaraki, Osaka 567-0047, Japan
E-mail: takeda@ist.osaka-u.ac.jp, sdate@ist.osaka-u.ac.jp

J. ZHANG and B. S. LEE

School of Computer Engineering, Nanyang Technological University,
Block N4, Nanyang Avenue 639798, Singapore
E-mail: jwzhang@ntu.edu.sg, ebslee@ntu.edu.sg

S. SHIMOJO

Osaka Research Center,
National Institute of Information and Communications Technology
and
Cybermedia Center, Osaka University,
5-1 Mihogaoka, Ibaraki, Osaka 567-0047, Japan
E-mail: shimojo@cmc.osaka-u.ac.jp

As the prevalence and coverage of grid deployment gather momentum, new tools are needed to support its effective operation and debugging. In this paper, we will introduce the design and implementation of our grid security monitoring tool, which enables multi-organization grid operation center to detect and visualize security abnormalities. Security sensors are deployed across the grid to collect security-related information from globus gatekeeper and jobmanager and store the information in a central database. The information is then visualized in an intelligent manner for security error/violation detection and resolution. The tool was successfully deployed and used across the Pacific Rim Application and Grid Middleware Association (PRAGMA) grid test-bed, where a variety of authentication and authorization failures were quickly detected and resolved. To ensure that the tool would be part of a set of tools for deployment at the Grid Operation Center, the tool was built as an extension module of the Multi-organizational Grid Accounting System (MOGAS), and shares some of the attributes used by other modules.

1. Introduction

Grid computing allows scientists to share computer resources distributed among multiple organizations. A number of international grid test-bed as well as production grid have been successfully deployed enabling/facilitating collaboration among scientists in various fields of science[1,2]. To realize large-scale collaboration, it is essential to have robust and flexible security mechanisms.

One can roughly categorize grid security into authentication and authorization. Authentication is the first phase, which is to identify user or host with credentials such as password or X.509 digital certificate. Authorization is the next phase that refers to whether the system permits or denies the request according to policies.

Grid researchers have studied security issues for a number of years. Thanks to their work, there are a number of middleware available to provide security in a grid environment. For example, globus toolkit[3], which is the current de facto standard grid middleware, has Grid Security Infrastructure (GSI)[4,5] as its security component. GSI provides sophisticated single sign-on functionality using proxy certificate which is an extension of X.509 certificate. However, existing grid middleware does not provide tools to monitor as well as visualize grid security (authentication and authorization) status across multiple organizations. In large-scale grid environment, it is very difficult for administrators to understand the status of grid security clearly and intuitively. Administrators need monitoring tools to quickly detect potential threats. Thus, the impetus of our project is to develop a grid security status monitoring tool to help grid administrators.

This paper consists as follows. Section 2 reviews some existing grid management and accounting tools to clarify the focus difference of our work from related works. In section 3, the design and implementation of our new tools are explained. In section 4, our visualization techniques of security information are introduced. Section 5 reports on our experience of deploying the tool across the PRAGMA grid test-bed. Finally, we conclude this paper in section 6.

2. Related Works

There are a variety of accounting and monitoring tools for clusters and grids. Table 1 summarizes some of these tools.

Ganglia[6] is a popular resource monitoring tool for clusters and grids. It collects resource information, such as CPU time and memory usage, from

Table 1.   Examples of existing accounting and monitoring tools.

	Environment	Purpose	Information
Ganglia	Cluster, grid	Resource monitoring	CPU time, memory usage
NVisionCC	Cluster	Security monitoring	Processes, ports, file integrity
APEL	Grid	Accounting	Job duration, parameters
DGAS	Grid	Accounting	Job duration, parameters
MOGAS	Grid	Accounting	Job duration, parameters
SCMSWeb	Grid	Resource monitoring	CPU time, memory usage.
Our interest	Grid	Security monitoring	Authentication, authorization

each cluster node and shows charts on its web interface. NVisionCC[7] is a security monitoring tool for clusters. It collects security information, such as running processes, open TCP/UDP ports and file integrity, and alerts problems on its web interface. These cluster monitoring tools assume and utilize resource homogeneity.

Accounting Processor for Event Logs (APEL)[8], Distributed Grid Accounting System (DGAS)[9] and Multi-organizational Grid Accounting System (MOGAS)[10,11] are accounting tools for grids and thus log user usage pattern. SCMSWeb[12], on the other hand, is a resource monitoring tool for grids, allowing the administrator to monitor the status and utilization of grid resources.

All the accounting tools above focus on logging the information about jobs. In our case, we are more interested in the security aspects of the grid, e.g. unsuccessful authentication/authorization of GSI and unusual log events. In our research, we develop a grid security monitoring tool to find global problems cannot be found with cluster tools. Security sensors are deployed at resource locations to collect security-related information from each resource. The tool visualizes security-related information to detect abnormal behavior quickly and easily.

3. Design and Implementation

As mentioned in section 2, accounting and monitoring tools collect information from each resource and visualize it. In our implementation, we have opted to extend MOGAS. Architecturally the system is as shown in figure 1.

Security sensors are deployed on the resource to detect access as well as security violation. As figure 1 shows, the architecture of MOGAS is

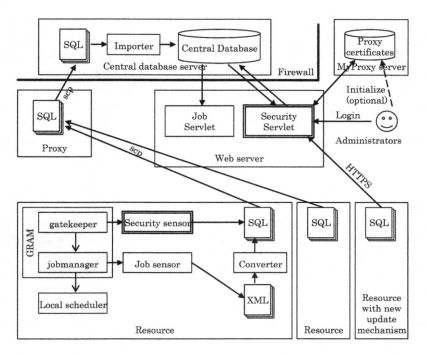

Figure 1.   Architecture of the security monitoring tool. Extended parts are highlighted with double lines.

centralized. It collects information from globus jobmanager of globus pre-WS GRAM[13]. Although pre-WS GRAM is the legacy implementation of GRAM, it is still widely used. Initially, the information is recorded in XML files. After that, they are converted into SQL scripts and uploaded onto the central database server via proxy server by using scp, which is file transfer functionality of Secure Shell (SSH). The central database server does not allow direct access from external hosts for security.

Firstly, we developed a sensor program to monitor and parse globus gatekeeper log file. As figure 1 shows, GRAM consists of gatekeeper and jobmanager. As authentication and authorization are performed at the gatekeeper, the job sensor of MOGAS is not able to collect security related information. The new sensor reads the gatekeeper log file periodically and creates SQL files for inserting records into the central database. It is written in Perl for portability and supports globus toolkit version 2, 3 and 4 series.

Secondly, the MOGAS database was extended to store gate-keeper events.   The most   important   table   in   the   database   is `globus_gatekeeper_session`. The information captured by the sensor is stored into this table. It has columns for time (GST), service distinguished name (DN) of X.509 certificate, service IP address, client IP address, user DN, authentication result, authorization result, mapped local account, requested service and invoked program. If the sensor is not able to parse log lines, the raw log messages are stored into `globus_gatekeeper_unexpected` table. We also added some tables to map distinguish names and IP addresses with organizations they belong. MOGAS and the new tool share the same MySQL database located at Nanyang Technological University, Singapore.

Thirdly, we developed a new web interface for security monitoring. The original web interface of MOGAS has no access control because resource usage ratio is open to public access. However, information included in gatekeeper logs is more sensitive. The new interface is independent of the original MOGAS interface and supports both password authentication and GSI authentication. An administrator is able to select authentication method at the login page. If he selects GSI method, the interface requests his proxy certificate to the specified MyProxy[14] server. It also has role-based access control (RBAC) mechanism for authorization. We developed a set of Java servlets on Tomcat version 5.5. Visualization techniques are described in detail in section 4.

Finally, we supported HTTPS based database update mechanism. In legacy scp-based update, SQL files are uploaded to the proxy server every 5 minutes, uploaded to the central server every 5 minutes, and then imported to the database every 5 minutes. It takes 15 minutes maximum and the delay is very long for monitoring. The new mechanism is much simpler. SQL files are uploaded to the web server every 1 minute, and then it directly updates the database. Basic authentication mechanism of HTTP is used to identify servers. Any command line HTTPS clients, such as popular GNU Wget, can be used.

4. Visualization of Security Information

Our new web interface has three views: graph view, table view and admin view. Graph view visualizes gatekeeper job request by drawing colored curves. Table view shows more detail information with tables and charts. Admin view is used for management of the web interface accounts and database.

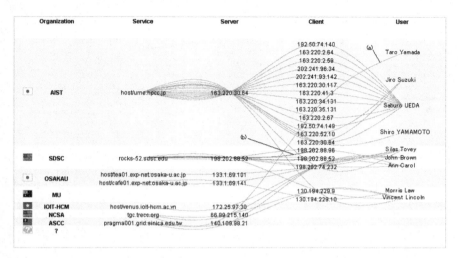

Figure 2. An example of graph shown in the graph view. User names are modified for privacy reasons.

Figure 2 is a snapshot of the graph view. It visualizes gatekeeper requests submitted in a specified period. The default period is the last 24 hours. A curve corresponds to a set of service, server, client and user in gatekeeper log. These four points are smoothly connected with a spline curve, because if they are connected with a polyline, multiple lines corresponding to different sets can overlap and cannot be distinguished. Green curves mean successful requests and red ones are authentication or authorization failures. For example, the green line (a) in figure 2 means that the user "Taro Yamada" submitted a successful job from the client "163.220.35.131" to the service "tgc.trecc.org" on the server "66.99.215.140". On the other hand, the red line (b) in figure 2 means that someone submitted an unsuccessful job from the client "198.202.88.96" to the service "rocks-52.sdsc.edu" on the server "198.202.88.52". In this case, the user is unknown because authentication failed. Entities (services, server, client and users) are sorted by organization they belong to. If an entity has not registered in the database, it is handled as unknown organization. By monitoring the graph view, administrators are able to understand the flows of job submissions at glance. If administrators find unusual flows or unknown entities, they should inspect what is happening by utilizing the detail information of table view. For example, if they find many unsuccessful requests to servers from a client, someone may be scanning ports to intrude.

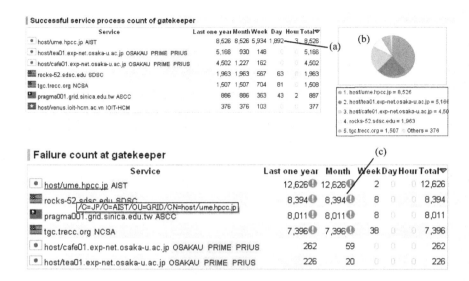

Figure 3.   Examples of tables and a chart shown in the table view.

Figure 3 is a snapshot of the table view. It visualizes both gatekeeper and jobmanager requests with tables, charts and icons. The layout and access control policy are defined in an XML file. The default layout has six tabs: statistics, failures, services, servers, clients and users. The statistics tab shows the number of successful job requests of each service and user with tables. For example, the number (a) in figure 3 means that 1,892 successful jobs were submitted to the service "host/ume.hpcc.jp" in last 24 hours. It also shows the ratio of requests with charts. The chart (b) in figure 3 shows the ratio of number of submitted successful jobs. The failure tab shows the number of failed jobs requests like statistics tab. The number (c) in figure 3 means that 8,394 unsuccessful jobs were submitted to the service "rocks-52.sdsc.edu". When the number of unsuccessful jobs exceeds the pre-defined threshold, an exclamation icon is indicated with the number to alert administrators. Both of statistics and failure tabs have links to the services, servers, clients and users tabs. For example, a user DN appears in the statistics tab is linked to the users tab. Administrators are able to find more detail and specific information by clicking links.

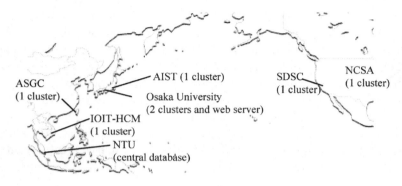

Figure 4. The test-bed environment.

5. An Experiment on the PRAGMA Grid Test-bed

We deployed the developed tool on the Pacific Rim Application and Grid Middleware Association (PRAGMA) grid test-bed. As of December 19, 2006, it had 361 hosts shared by 27 organizations in 14 countries. First, we installed the sensor to monitor gatekeeper log on seven master nodes of clusters. Two of them were located at Osaka University, Japan, and rests of them were at National Institute of Advanced Industrial Science and Technology (AIST/Japan), Academia Sinica Grid Computing Center (ASGC/Taiwan), HCMC Institute of Information Technology (IOIT-HCM/Vietnam), National Center for Supercomputing Applications (NCSA/USA) and San Diego Supercomputer Center (SDSC/USA). All of them support pre-WS GRAM as one of services. We set up the web interface on a server in Osaka University. The central database was located at Nanyang Technological University (NTU/Singapore) and connected with the web server via VPN. Geographical locations are shown in figure 4.

Since August 2006, we have monitored the behavior of grid by using the tool. When we found unknown entities, we added them into database after inspection. Sometimes, they were temporarily allocated IP addresses for conference. As the web interface indicates question icons for unknown entities, administrators were able to find unusual ones easily.

Most of the authentication failures we found were caused by wrong certificates. For example, some users tried to use expired certificates or certificates only valid for local use. Some users did not have required CA certificates for clients. A few number of authentication failures were at protocol level and seemed to be caused by network problems. Authorization failures we found were grid-map failures. Some users tried to access unauthorized hosts or to use wrong certificates by mistake. We also found some abnormal behavior caused by software bugs by watching the `globus_gatekeeper_unexpected` table. We did not find any suspicious trial from uncertain clients in the period. We could know that each host we monitored had a strict firewall and they were properly working.

Through this experiment, we found that a few number of users caused most of log events in this test-bed. They submitted thousands of simple jobs (or test jobs) using shell scripts. In this case, it is difficult to find significant events without tools like this.

6. Conclusion and Future Works

We have been developing a new security monitoring tool aiming to help grid and site administrators. We have extended MOGAS, which is an existing grid accounting system, to show security information on a new web interface. We have deployed it on a grid test-bed and confirmed that it is greatly helpful for administrators to find problems and possible threats in multi-organizational grid.

The current implementation only supports globus pre-WS GRAM. We are planning to develop more sensors to support more services, such as WS GRAM, GridFTP, UNIX syslog and the web interface itself. We are also planning to improve the web interface in usability, scalability and flexibility of access control.

Acknowledgments

We would like to thank PRAGMA members for their assistance in the deployment of the security sensors across the international grid test-bed. MOGAS was initially funded by National Grid Office Singapore. A part of this research is supported by the Foresting of Globally-leading Researchers in Integrated Science (PRIUS) promoted by Osaka University under the MEXT framework of University Education Internationalization Program.

References

1. Enabling Grids for E-science (EGEE), `http://public.eu-egee.org/`.
2. Open Science Grid (OSG), `http://www.opensciencegrid.org/`.
3. I. Foster. Globus Toolkit Version 4: Software for Service-Oriented Systems. *IFIP International Conference on Network and Parallel Computing, Springer-Verlag LNCS 3779*, pp 2-13 (2006).

4. I. Foster, C. Kesselman, G. Tsudik, and S. Tuecke. A Security Architecture for Computational Grids. *Proceedings of 5th ACM Conference on Computer and Communications Security Conference,* pp. 83–92 (1998).
5. V. Welch, F. Siebenlist, I. Foster, J. Brresnahan, K. Czajkowski, J. Gawor, C. Kesselman, S. Meder, L. Pearlman and S. Tuedke. Security for Grid Services. *Twelfth International Symposium on High Performance Distributed Computing (HPDC-12)* (2003).
6. M. L. Massie, B. N. Chun and D. E. Culler. The Ganglia Distributed Monitoring System: Design, Implementation, and Experience. *Parallel Computing,* Vol. 30, Issue 7 (2004).
7. W. Yurcik, X. Meng and N. Kiyanclar. NVisionCC: A Visualization Framework for High Performance Cluster Security. *Proceedings of the 2004 ACM workshop on Visualization and data mining for computer security,* pp. 133–137 (2004).
8. R. Byroma, R. Cordenonsib, L. Cornwalla, M. Craiga, A. Djaouia, A. Duncana, S. Fishera, J. Gordona, S. Hicksa, D. Kanta, J. Leakec, R. Middletona, M. Thorpea, J. Walka and A. Wilson. APEL: An Implementation of Grid Accounting Using R-GMA. *UK e-Science All Hands Conference, Nottingham, 19th–22nd* (2005).
9. R. M. Piro, A. Guarise and A. Werbrouck. An Economy-based Accounting Infrastructure for the DataGrid. *Proceedings of the 4th International Workshop on Grid Computing (GRID2003), Phoenix, Arizona (USA),* (2003).
10. D. Lim, Q. T. Ho, J. Zhang, B. S. Lee and Y. S. Ong. MOGAS: A Multi-Organisation Grid Accounting System. *International Journal of Information Technology,* Vol.11, No 4, pp. 84–103.
11. B. S. Lee, M. Tang, J. Zhang, O. Y. Soon, C. Zheng, P. Arzberger and D. Abramson. Analysis of Jobs in a Multi-Organisation Grid test-bed, *Proceedings of the Sixth IEEE International Symposium on Cluster Computing and Grid Workshops* (2006).
12. OpenSCE Project, http://www.opensce.org/.
13. K. Czajkowski, I. Foster, N. Karonis, C. Kesselman, S. Martin, W. Smith, and S. Tuecke. A Resource Management Architecture for Metacomputing Systems. *Proceedings of IPPS/SPDP '98 Workshop on Job Scheduling Strategies for Parallel Processing,* pp. 62–82 (1998).
14. J. Novotny, S. Tuecke and V. Welch. An Online Credential Repository for the Grid: MyProxy. *Proceedings of the Tenth International Symposium on High Performance Distributed Computing (HPDC-10),* IEEE Press (2001).

Grid Applications

DISTRIBUTED AUTOMATIC FRAME GENERATION FOR CARTOON ANIMATION[*]

SEAH HOCK SOON[1], TIAN FENG, LU YIXIANG, QIU JIE and CHEN QUAN

School of Computer Engineering
Nanyang Technological University, Singapore
[1]Email: ashsseah@ntu.edu.sg

Drawing intermediate frames, so called inbetweens, is a very time consuming and labor-intensive task in the production of cartoon animation. Many approaches have been investigated to automate the inbetweening process. In this paper we propose a distributed rendering solution for inbetweening based on our novel modeling method, Disk B-spline.Curve The experimental results show that, compared to a single workstation, the cluster based framework provides much better performance with more than 85% of time being saved. Moving forward, we believe that the Grid will be an ideal solution to improve the animation productivity further in the future.

1. Introduction

Traditionally, 2D animation production has been a labor-intensive artisan process of building up animated sequences entirely by hand. With script, story-board and character design and exposure sheets, animators draw keyframes showing the major features of each character's action and assistant animators produce inbetweens to yield a smooth animation. These line drawings will be subsequently painted. Frames of different layers are combined into composite frames which appear in the final animation according to the exposure sheets. Among various procedures, inbetween drawing and coloring are the most tedious tasks.

To save time and labor, an automatic inbetweening algorithm and system is desirable. Much research has since been done on interpolation of keyframes. For example, [1] and [2] work on image morphing using triangulation. This is not suitable for line drawings. A pre-defined correspondence between components, e.g. points, curves or shapes, [3, 4, 5], in two keyframes is usually needed to deliver smoother and better looking intermediate images. However, this requires

---

[*]The work is partially supported by Singapore A*Star Grant (052 015 0024).

much user-interaction beforehand. Some methods of automatic correspondence [6] work well for simple cases where the number of components to be matched is small but usually user-correction is hardly avoidable. J. D. Fekete *et al.* [7] presented an approach to a complete vectorized drawing process by providing an interface for a "paperless" system. He noticed that the automation changes the nature of inbetweening and limits it complexity. In this paper we present an interpolation approach based on our novel 2D representation model, Disk B-spline Curve (DBSC). Corresponding strokes, whose skeleton and width are modeled by DBSC, of two or more keyframes are automatically interpolated to generate natural and accurate inbetweens.

Automatic inbetween generation cuts down the time and cost of animation production. However, given the fact that a 90-minute animation feature may easily consist of more than dozens of thousands of keyframes, the generation of inbetween remains a time consuming and computation-intensive process. In addition, animations are created from a number of layers for characters, backgrounds, and other elements, and each layer has to be rendered separately. Hence many 3D animation companies build their own render farms, which are clusters of interconnected computers. There are some commercial render farms available online, such as ResPower [8] and RenderIt [9]. Going beyond the cluster and reducing the rendering time further, the Grid Computing, or simply called Grid, is introduced and realized by linking up clusters across different locations or areas. Grid computing may help smaller companies compete with bigger players in major markets. One such example is AXYZ Animation Inc. [10], a Toronto-based firm with 35 employees, creating special effects for TV ads. The Sun's Grid Engine [11] gives the company smoother workflow and better control of projects.

While most Grid applications focus on 3D CGI and rendering, we propose in this paper a distributed 2D animation rendering framework by leveraging on our inbetweening technology. First, animators vectorize and decompose keyframes into a number of layers to build correspondences of strokes when occlusion occurs. The framework then allows the animators to submit layers of keyframes to a cluster through their own workstations. The cluster will handle two tasks, inbetween generation and composition of various layers. Subsequently, the final rendering results, i.e. a sequence of frames (including composite keyframes and inbetweens), are sent back to animator for them to view at their workstations and touch-up if necessary. Our experimental results show that the framework is not only able to increase the speed of frame generation and thus the productivity of animation, but also provide animators nearly simultaneous feedback on the quality of frames. Moving forward, we will extend this framework from cluster to the Grid, which we believe will impact the whole 2D animation industry.

In the rest of the paper the details of DBSC and inbetweening technology are briefly introduced first. Then, we will give details on the rendering framework, including both algorithm and implementation, in the Section 3. Following experiment results in the Section 4, the conclusion and future work are given at the end of the paper.

2. Stroke Representation with Disk B-Spine Curve and Inbetweening

Disk B-spline curve (DBSC) is a novel 2D stroke representation approach [12]. It is defined as $<D>(t) = \sum_{i=0}^{n} N_{i,p}(t) < P_i; r_i >$, where P_i are control points, r_i are control radii and $N_{i,p}(t)$ is the ith B-spline basis of degree p with knot vector $[u_0,...,u_m] = \{a,...a,u_{p+1},...,u_{m-p-1},b...,b\}$. With this, we can define properties and algorithms of DBSC as shown in Figure 1. More details can be found in Ref. 12.

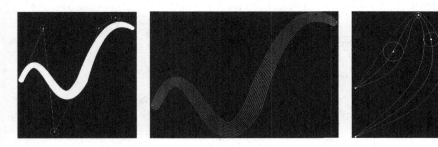

Fig. 1. Definition of Disk B-spline Curve.

DBSC can be applied to interpolate two or more keyframes [12]. We assume the two DBSCs have the same degree, same number of control points and same knot vector i.e. $<D_1>(t) = \sum_{i=0}^{n} N_{i,p}(t) < P_i; r_i >$, $<D_2>(t) = \sum_{i=0}^{n} N_{i,p}(t) < Q_i; s_i >$ and the knot vector T. The inbetween DBSCs can then be generated by interpolating $<D_1>$ and $<D_2>$'s corresponding control points and radii. An example of inbetweening is shown in Figure 2.

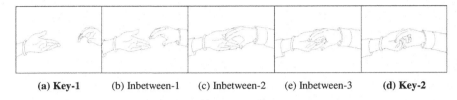

(a) **Key-1**   (b) Inbetween-1   (c) Inbetween-2   (e) Inbetween-3   (d) **Key-2**

Fig. 2. Example of inbetweening with DBSC.

3. Frame Generation Framework

To cut down the rendering time for 3D CGI, many companies either build their render farms, or use the commercial online farms, or adopt the Grid computing. Similarly, we propose a frame generation framework for 2D animation production, aiming to increase animator's productivity and allowing them to focus more time on creativity work rather than labor-intensive drawing task. The framework is based on the concept of a cluster for distributed computing and its structure is illustrated below in Figure 3.

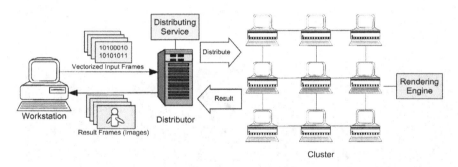

Fig. 3. Distributed Rendering Framework.

First, an animator works on the *client program* running in the *Workstation* to decompose key frames into layers (if necessary), vectorizes and corresponds strokes of the key frames. After the button *"render by server"* in the *client program* is clicked, all strokes together with other data (layer, DBSC, etc.) are then serialized, compressed and streamed over local network to the distributor. In the mean time the *client program* is locked so that no further change can be made to the animation sequence before the rendering result is received. Upon receiving the rendering request, the *distributing service* on the *distributor* analyzes the work load, divides the task into subtasks and distributes them to the *cluster* nodes. Each node has already been pre-loaded with our 2D animation *rendering engine*, which consists of two main modules, inbetweening and merging. The *distributor* waits until every node completes its tasks and sends back the results, and then streams them back to the animator who has submitted the rendering request.

When the rendering job (inbetweening and merging) is completed in the *cluster*, a sequence of frames (in the form of raster images) is sent back to the *workstation*. Here, the images are compressed and represented in the PNG (portable network graphics) format, which is the best format for 2D animation, because 2D animation frames are usually very limited in colors and have a large area of white background before they are colored or composed with background.

3.1. *Rendering Algorithm and Complexity*

An animation sequence is represented as a collection of layers. A layer contains a set of frames; and a frame in turn is comprised of strokes, which can be combined into groups if necessary. So a sequence can be considered as a matrix of strokes, as shown in (1), where N_S and N_F are the numbers of strokes and composite frames respectively. S_{ij} denotes the ith stroke in the jth composite frame.

$$
\begin{bmatrix}
S_{11} & S_{12} & \cdots & S_{1N_F} \\
S_{21} & S_{22} & \cdots & S_{2N_F} \\
\cdots & \cdots & \cdots & \cdots \\
S_{N_S1} & S_{N_S2} & \cdots & S_{N_SN_F}
\end{bmatrix}
\tag{1}
$$

Each column of the matrix constitutes a composite frame, and each row represents a set of corresponded strokes, which is defined as CS_i in this paper. The rendering process of 2D animation consists of two main tasks: inbetweening (or interpolation) and merging, which are shown in Table 1,

Table 1. Rendering Process.

Render (…)	

For each set of corresponded strokes CS_i in the animation
  For each pair of successive strokes in CS_i
    Generate given number of inbetween strokes
	Inbetweening

For each composite frame F_j in the animation
  Create a buffer image *buf* with specified output dimension
  For each frame *f* in F_j
    Remove occluded strokes or stroke segments
    Merge *f* with *buf* (performance is proportional to output dimension)
	Merging

where CS_i denotes the ith set of corresponded strokes $\{S_{ij}, j = 1, 2...N_F\}$, and F_j is the jth composite frame. An example of the interpolation and merging process is illustrated below.

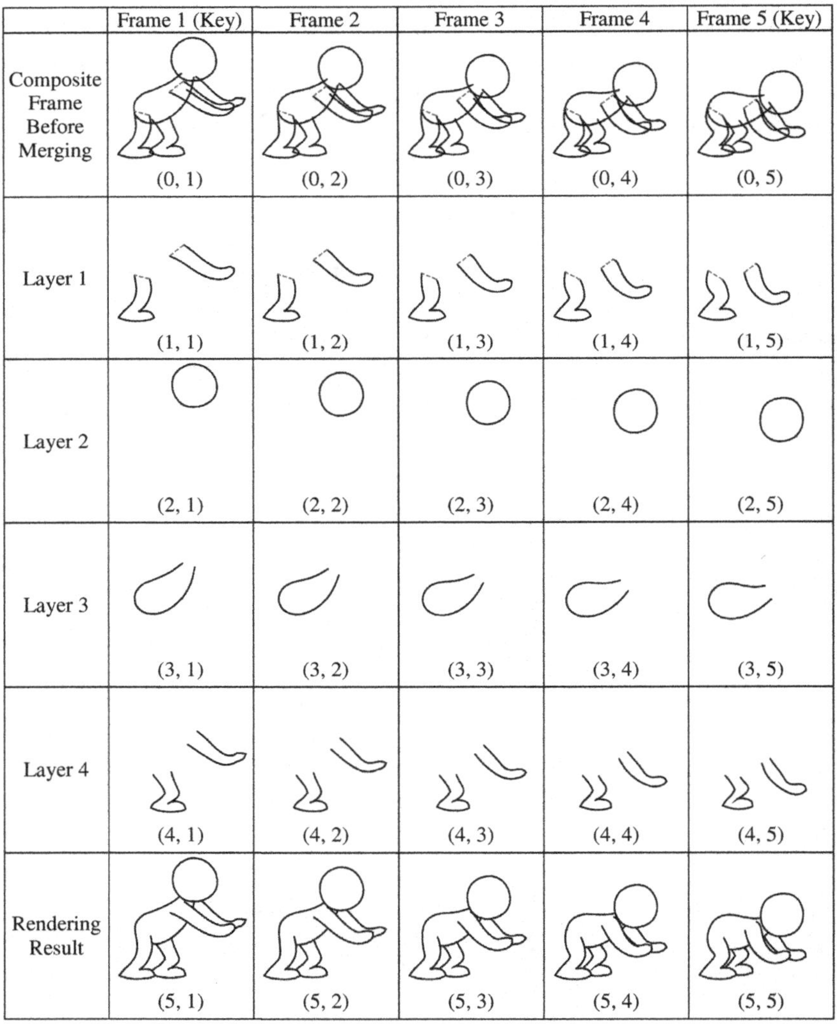

	Frame 1 (Key)	Frame 2	Frame 3	Frame 4	Frame 5 (Key)
Composite Frame Before Merging	(0, 1)	(0, 2)	(0, 3)	(0, 4)	(0, 5)
Layer 1	(1, 1)	(1, 2)	(1, 3)	(1, 4)	(1, 5)
Layer 2	(2, 1)	(2, 2)	(2, 3)	(2, 4)	(2, 5)
Layer 3	(3, 1)	(3, 2)	(3, 3)	(3, 4)	(3, 5)
Layer 4	(4, 1)	(4, 2)	(4, 3)	(4, 4)	(4, 5)
Rendering Result	(5, 1)	(5, 2)	(5, 3)	(5, 4)	(5, 5)

Fig. 4. Rendering Process Decomposed.

As shown in Figure 4, each composite frame $(0, m)$ is composed of four layers, and the frame at each layer n is represented as frame (n, m), where n and m are the indices of layers and frames respectively. For example, frame $(0, 1)$ is the composition of frames $(1, 1)$, $(2, 1)$, $(3, 1)$ and $(4, 1)$. Frames $(n, 1)$ and $(n, 5)$ are the input key frames, which are interpolated to obtain inbetween frames at each layer. After inbetweening, each frame $(5, m)$ is obtained by merging frames $(1, m)$ and $(4, m)$. The rendering results are illustrated as frames $(5, 1)$ to $(5, 5)$.

Obviously the total number of composite frames is computed based on the key and inbetween frames:

$$N_F = N_{KF} + (N_{KF} - 1) \times N_{IB} \tag{2}$$

where N_F, N_{KF} and N_{IB} are total numbers of composite frames, keyframes, and inbetween frames between each pair of consecutive keyframes respectively.

According to the pseudo code in Table 1, the time complexity of the inbetweening algorithm is computed as:

$$C_{interpolate} = O(N_S \times (N_{KF} - 1) \times N_{IB}) \tag{3}$$

where N_S is the number of strokes in each composite frame.

Equation (3) can be further deducted as:

$$\begin{aligned} C_{interpolate} &= O\left(N_S \times (N_{KF} - 1) \times \frac{N_F - N_{KF}}{N_{KF} - 1} \right) \\ &= O(N_S \times (N_F - N_{KF})) \\ &= O(N_S \times N_F) \end{aligned} \tag{4}$$

The merging algorithm processes each composite frame as an individual entity. The processing time of each composite frame is determined by the output dimension and the number of composite frames and their resolution. So its time complexity can be computed as follows:

$$C_{merge} = O(N_L \times N_F \times W \times H) \tag{5}$$

where N_L, N_F are the numbers of layers and composite frames, W and H are the width and height of the frames in pixel, respectively.

According to the above analysis, the overall time complexity of the rendering algorithm is:

$$C_{non-distrib} = C_{interpolate} + C_{merge} = O(N_S \times N_F + N_L \times N_F \times W \times H) \qquad (6)$$

3.2. Distributed Rendering Algorithm

The distributed rendering algorithm, introduced in the previous section, distribute different tasks into the distributor and nodes, as shown in Table 2.

Table 2. Distributed Rendering Algorithm.

Render (...)	

Distributor distributes corresponded stroke sets to available nodes evenly
On each **node**,
  For each set of corresponded strokes CS_i assigned to this node
    For each pair of successive strokes in CS_i
      Generate given number of inbetween strokes
	Inbetweening

For each composite frame F_j in the animation
Distributor picks a cluster node to merge F_j
On each **node**,
  Create a buffer image *buf* with specified output dimension
  For each frame f in F_j
    Remove occluded strokes or stroke segments
    Merge f with *buf* (performance is proportional to output dimension)
	Merging

The time complexity of the distributed rendering algorithm is determined by the computation and the communication time. Given the large amount of images typically sent, the network setup time and latency are relatively quite small. So the main communication time is the frame transferring time between the client workstation and the cluster. Accordingly, the overall time complexity for the distributed rendering algorithm is:

$$C_{distribute} = C_{compute} + C_{transfer} \qquad (7)$$

Similar to the non-distributed, the overall computational complexity is composed of interpolation complexity and merging complexity.

$$C_{compute} = C_{distrib\_interpolate} + C_{distrib\_merge} \qquad (8)$$

Assume N_N denotes number of nodes in the cluster, each node will be assigned with $\frac{N_S}{N_N}$ sets of corresponding strokes. Therefore, the time complexity for interpolation is computed as:

$$C_{distrib\_interpolate} = O\left(\frac{N_S \times N_F}{N_N}\right) \tag{9}$$

Similarly, the time complexity for merging the entire sequence is:

$$C_{distrib\_merge} = O\left(\frac{N_F \times N_L \times W \times H}{N_N}\right) \tag{10}$$

The overall time complexity of the distributed rendering algorithm is hence calculated as:

$$C_{compute} = C_{distrib\_interpolate} + C_{distrib\_merge} = O\left(\frac{N_S N_F + N_F N_L \times W \times H}{N_N}\right) \tag{11}$$

The time spent on sending vectorized strokes is determined by the numbers of key frames (N_{KF}) and strokes in each composite frames (N_S) in the sequence.

$$C_{send} = O(N_{KF} \times N_S) \tag{12}$$

The frames sent back is a sequence of raster images, so the receiving time is determined by the total number of frames and the size of each frame which is related to the output resolution.

$$C_{receive} = O(N_F \times W \times H) \tag{13}$$

Based on Equation (12) and (13), the time complexity for transferring is obtained as:

$$\begin{aligned} C_{transfer} &= C_{send} + C_{receive} \\ &= O_{send}(N_{KF} \times N_S) + O_{receive}(N_F \times W \times H) \end{aligned} \tag{14}$$

The overall time complexity for the distributed rendering algorithm is thus computed as:

$$C_{distribute} = O_{compute}\left(\frac{N_S N_F + N_F N_L \times W \times H}{N_N}\right)$$
$$+O_{send}(N_F \times N_S) + O_{receive}(N_F \times W \times H)$$

$$(15)$$

4. Experimental Results

The experiment is carried out with an internal cluster of 7 nodes. Each node is equipped with Intel Xeon 3.2 Processor and 3G of RAM. A distributor server, with 2 Intel Core Duo 3.0G Processors and 2G of RAM, is also setup, by installing an ad hoc distributing service for interactive rendering on it. The client workstation is configured with Intel Core Duo 3.2G processor and 2G of RAM.

4.1. *Sample Output*

The distributed rendering service is tested with two examples, Tukasa and Sayuri. The following are the sample outputs, where key frames are marked with a dark boarder.

4.1.1. *Tukasa Rendering Case*

In Figure 5, the first and last images are the merging result of the two input key frames while the rest are generated from the two key frames and then merged.

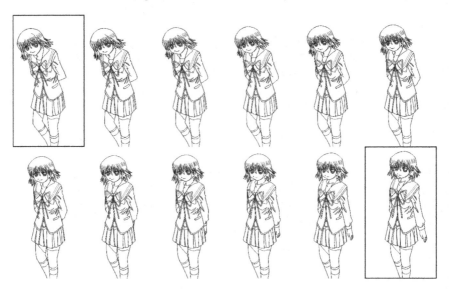

Fig. 5. Tukasa: Rendering Output (Courtesy of Animation International Co. Inc.).

The details of this animation sequence and rendering time are shown in the table below. It can be seen that, with the cluster the rendering time is reduced to 13.85% of what otherwise is done in a single workstation.

Table 3. Tukasa – Rendering Details and Performance.

Layers	Key Frames	Total Frames	Strokes	Output Dimension (Pixels)	Client Rendering Time (Seconds)	Distributed Rendering Time (Seconds)
11	2	12	348	2000×488	115.382	15.985

4.1.2. *Sayuri Rendering Case*

The following is the rendering result of Sayuri case. There are 5 key frames and 10 inbetweens for each pair of key frames. Instead of showing all 45 frames, we sample some inbetween frame for illustration purpose. The frame, IB12_5 denotes the fifth inbetween generated for the key frames Key1 and Key2; IB23_3 represents the third inbetween for the key frame Key 2 and Key3, etc.

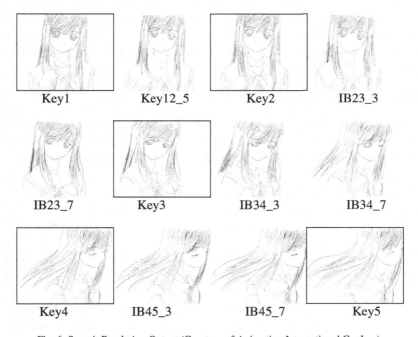

Fig. 6. Sayuri: Rendering Output (Courtesy of Animation International Co. Inc.).

The details of this sequence and rendering time are shown below.

Table 4. Sayuri: Rendering Details and Performance.

Layers	Key Frames	Total Frames	Strokes	Output Dimension (Pixels)	Client Rendering Time (Seconds)	Distributed Rendering Time (Seconds)
12	5	45	381	1000×812	184.232	27.283

Given total 45 output frames, the distributed rendering takes less than half a minute, which is acceptable as an interactive function.

5. Conclusion and Future Work

An automatic inbetween generation algorithm and framework is proposed, aiming to cut down the production time of cartoon animation. The keyframes represented by DBSC are interpolated to generate a number of inbetweens as required by users. A framework on distributed frame generation is proposed and tested with several Japanese Anime sequences. The result analysis concludes that a cluster can improve the rendering performance by more than 85%.

Going further, we will be using the Grid for our inbetweening algorithm. Apart from inbetweening, in the future we will add an auto coloring process into the cluster and the Grid subsequently.

References

1. Alexa M, Cohen-Or D, Levin D. As-rigid-as-possible shape interpolation. In *Proceedings of the 27th Annual Conference on Computer Graphics and Interactive Techniques*, pages 157–164. ACM Press/Addison-Wesley Publishing Co., 2000.
2. Van den Bergh J,Di Fiore F, Claes J, Van Reeth F. Interactively morphing irregularly shaped images employing subdivision techniques. In *1st Ibero-American Symposium on Computer Graphics 2002 (SIACG 2002)*. XX: XYQ2, 2002; 315–321.
3. Bartel RH and Hardock RT. Curve-to-Curve Associations in Spline-Based Inbetweening and Sweeping. In *Proceedings of the 1989 ACM SIGGRAPH conference*, pages 167–174, 1989.
4. Sederberg T W and Greenwood E. Shape Blending of 2-D Piecewise Curves. In *Mathematical methods for curves and surfaces*, Vanderbilt University Press, pages 497–506, 1999.

5. Alexa M, Cohen-Or D, and Levin D. As-rigidas-possible shape interpolation. In *Proceedings of the 27th annual conference on Computer graphics and interactive techniques*, pages 157–164. ACM Press/Addison-Wesley Publishing Co., 2000.

6. Kort A. Computer Aided Inbetweening. In *ACM Press*, 2002.

7. Fekete J. D., Bizouarn E., Cournarie E., Galas T., Taillefer F. TicTacToon: a paperless system for professional 2D animation. In *Computer Graphics Proceedings*, Annual Conference Series, pages 79–90, 1995.

8. http://www.respower.com

9. http://www.render-it.co.uk

10. http://www.axyzfx.com

11. http://www.sun.com/software/Gridware/index.xml

12. Wu Z K, Seah H S, Tian F, Xiao X, Xie B Y, "Artistic Brushstroke Representation and Animation with Disk B-Spline Curve", *ACM SIGCHI International Conference on Advances in Computer Entertainment Technology*, ACE 2005, Jun 2005, Spain.

154

PHENOTYPE GENOTYPE EXPLORATION ON A DESKTOP GPU GRID*

CHEN CHEN, AARTI SINGH, WEIGUO LIU and KARL-WOLFGANG
MÜLLER-WITTIG

School of Computer Engineering,
Nanyang Technological University, Singapore 639798,
E-mail: { cchen, aarti, liuweiguo, askwmwittig} @ntu.edu.sg

W. MITCHELL

Genome Institute of Singapore,
60 Biopolis Street, #02-01, Genome, Singapore 138672,
E-mail: mitchellw@gis.a-star.edu.sg

BERTIL SCHMIDT

University of New South Wales Asia,
Level 7 North, 1 Kay Siang Rd, Singapore 248922,
E-mail: Bertil.Schmidt@unswasia.edu.sg

Comparative genomics provides a powerful tool for studying evolutionary changes among organisms. We have designed a new tool, called *Phenotype Genotype Explorer* to nominate candidate genes responsible for a given phenotype. There are huge datasets involved which makes this approach impractical on traditional computer architectures leading to prohibitively long runtimes. In this paper, We present a computational architecture based on a desktop grid environment and and commodity graphics hardware to significantly accelerate the comparative genomics application. We present the deployment and evaluation of this approach on our grid testbed for the comparison of microbial genomes.

1. Introduction

High-throughput techniques for DNA sequencing have led to an enormous growth in the amount of publicly available genomic data. Presently, 453 complete genome sequences are available and another 1686 genome-sequencing projects are in progress.[1] As the sequences of more and more

---

*The work was supported by the A*Star BMRC research grant no. 04/1/22/19/375.

genomes become available, we have reached a critical mass where, instead of focusing on a subset of sequences, we can use entire genome data sets to derive global inferences and metadata.

Comparative genomics refers to the study of relationships between the genomes of different species or strains. It is currently being used for ortholog detection,[8] bacterial pharmacogenomics,[6] clustering of similar protein sequences,[7] etc. Unfortunately, comparative genomics applications are highly computationally intensive tasks due to the large sequence data sets involved and typically take a few months to complete. These runtime requirements are likely to become even more severe due to the rapid growth in the size of genomic databases.

In this paper we present the design of PheGee (Phenotype Genotype Explorer), a new comparative genomics tool that nominates candidate genes responsible for a certain phenotype π given sets of phenotype positive $(\pi+)$ and phenotype negative $(\pi-)$ species.

We propose hybrid computational architecture based on a grid platform and further that can be efficiently applied on GPUs (Graphics Processing Units) to comparative genomics. The driving force and motivation behind this architecture is the price/performance ratio. Using desktop grids as in the volunteer computing approach is currently one of the most efficient and simple ways to gain supercomputer power for a reasonable price. Installing in addition massively parallel processor add-on boards such as modern computer graphics cards within each desktop can further improve the cost/performance ratio significantly.

To achieve grid task parallelism we choose the open source BOINC (Berkeley Open Infrastructure for Network Computing[2]) framework. The power and mass appeal of volunteer computing for implementing task parallel problems has been demonstrated in projects like SETI@home[4] and Predictor@home[17] which are based on BOINC.

Coarse-grained Parallelism is achieved by intelligently distributing the task assigned by the BOINC server to processors on host computers. Modern hardware such as multi-core CPUs and GPUs offer cost-effective solutions to many problems. In particular, the GPU is suitable to solve parallel floating point computing problem. Therefore, GPGPU (General-Purpose computation on a GPU) is an active area of researchs in high performance computing.[10,12,13]

The rest of this paper is organized as follows. Section 2 presents the design of PheGee. The efficient mapping of comparative genomics applications onto this new architecture is presented in Section 3. Deployment and performance evaluation are presented in Section 4. Section 5 analyzes the results of a comparative study of microbial genomes by PheGee. Finally, Section 6 concludes the paper.

2. Design of Phenotype Genotype Explorer

The main goal of comparative genomics is to study evolutionary changes among organisms. These changes are then used to identify genes that are conserved among species, as well as genes that give each organism its unique characteristics. Phenotype genotype exploration is an approach that makes use of the results of an all-against-all genome comparison to nominate candidate genes responsible for a phenotype π given user specified sets of phenotype positive $(\pi+)$ and phenotype negative $(\pi-)$ species for which whole genome sequences are available to user biologists.

PheGee exploits the simple observation: Given a set of species, A, which evince a particular phenotype, π, and a second set of species, B, which do not evince π, then in general genes responsible for π will be present in A and absent from B. Given incomplete knowledge, in the universe of sequenced organisms there will be a third set, C, generally the largest of the three, comprising those organisms undefined in terms of π. To cast this in symbolic terms, if a particular process is the outcome of three genes $x \rightarrow y \rightarrow z$, then in general homologs of x, y, and z will be found in A but not in B. Those genes found in all members of A and not found in B, are therefore the best candidates for genes responsible for the process resulting from x, y, z. However, a perfect concordance between phenotype and genotype in sets of organisms is not guaranteed. Apart from epigenetic and environmental factors that can shape phenotype, the following genetic phenomena might disrupt the relationship.

- **Gene Replacement:** Gene y can be lost in some members of A, say A^*. In A^* the function of y may have been replaced by some other gene, w.
- **Horizontal Gene Transfer:** Genes x, y, or z may be adopted by a new species through the process of *horizontal gene transfer*. In this scenario some members of B, say B^*, will contain a gene correctly associated with phenotype π, even though no member of B evinces the phenotype.
- **Function driven by small protein motif:** A third source of ambiguity emerges in the case of proteins where biochemical function is driven by a relatively small motif, with the bulk of the protein evolving freely. This situation can produce genes which are functionally linked to phenotype π,

but which will only be identified as homologs by very sensitive sequence analysis methods.

- **Systemic convergent evolution:** The phenotype chosen to parse the species may not be genetically *pure*. Partitioning species according to the observed phenotype then will create a genetically mixed set of $\pi+$ organisms.

Because of the above processes a useful identification of gene candidates for a given genotype cannot demand that each $\pi+$ genome contains a homolog of the same $\pi+$ linked gene, or that every $\pi-$ genome lack all $\pi+$ linked genes. Each absence of a homology in a $\pi+$ genome, or presence of a $\pi+$ homolog in a $\pi-$ genome, can be termed an 'exception'. One way to prioritize groups of homolog candidates is by the number of exceptions generated for a all given genes for a given $\pi+/\pi-$ partition. Despite the exceptions, we think that a phenotype to genotype strategy can successfully identify underlying genetic structure given that reasonably large numbers of sample genomes are available. The $\pi+/\pi-$ partition is computed using the following method:

- **INPUT:** A number of n genomes $G_1,\ldots,G_n$ and a set of $n(n-1)/2$ distance matrices $D(i,j)$ as described in Section 5. Additionally, the given genomes are divided into a phenotype positive set $\pi+ = \{G_1,\ldots,G_m\}$ and a phenotype negative set $\pi- = \{G_{m+1},\ldots,G_n\}$.
- **OUTPUT:** All genes $g_{i,k}$ with the maximal partitioning score $P(g_{i,k})$ among all genes.
- **METHOD:** The partitioning score $P(g_{i,k})$ is computed for each gene, $1 \leq i \leq n$, $1 \leq k \leq \phi(i)$, as follows.

  - **Case 1:** $G_i \in \pi+$; i.e. the given gene is part of a phenotype positive genome. Then the best match of the gene in the phenotype negative set $(g_{i,k})$ is identified, which is calculated by finding the smallest E-value in the distance matrix:

$$\epsilon(g_{i,k}) = \min_{m+1 \leq j \leq n, 1 \leq l \leq \phi(j)} d(g_{i,k}, g_{j,l})$$

This value is then used as a threshold to determine partitioning score $P(g_{i,k})$, which is the number of genomes in $\pi+$ that contain a matching gene better than this score:

$$P(g_{i,k}) = \frac{\sum_{j=1}^{m} \delta(g_{i,k}, j, \epsilon(g_{i,k}))}{m}$$

where

$$\delta(g_{i,k}, j, \epsilon(g_{i,k})) = \begin{cases} 1 & if \quad \min_{1 \le l \le \phi(j)} d(g_{i,k}, g_{j,l}) \le \epsilon(g_{i,k}) \\ 0 & otherwise \end{cases}$$

- **Case 2:** $G_i \in \pi-$: similar (but with positive and negative sets interchanged and n replaced by $n - m$)

3. Mapping of Comparative Genomics onto the Hybrid Grid Architecture

In order to compare two gene sequences we have decided on using E-values computed from pairwise local sequence alignments scores as distances. The pairwise alignment score is computed by the Smith-Waterman algorithm.[15] The choice of the Smith-Waterman algorithm is motivated by its superior sensitivity for low-scoring alignment[5] as compared to other, faster algorithms such as BLAST.[3]

Given a number of n genomes G_1, ..., G_n with genome i containing $\phi(i)$ genes, i.e. $G_i = \{g_{i,1}, \ldots, g_{i,\phi(i)}\}$, where $g_{i,k}$ denotes the kth gene of genome i. The result of the all-against-all comparison can then be described as a set of $n(n-1)/2$ distance matrix $D(i,j)$ of size $\phi(i) \times \phi(j)$ containing all pairwise distances $d(g_{i,k}, g_{j,l})$, $1 \le k \le \phi(i)$, $1 \le l \le \phi(j)$, for each pair of genes $g_{i,k}$ and $g_{j,l}$ in genome i and genome j. This all-against-all comparison can be mapped onto our hybrid grid architecture as follows:

- splitting the problem into smaller chunks of all-against-all comparison tasks (task parallelization) at the server end.
- processing these smaller tasks by calculating the individual Smith Waterman scores at the client end (data parallelization), which can be implemented in a data parallel manner on GPU and sequential manner on CPUs.

3.1. *Task Parallelization Using BOINC*

The various considerations that need to be taken into account at the server end for implementing the task parallelization are as follows:

(1) *The input data files for the client application should be optimized for the GPU code.* The GPU code runs optimally if all the sequences in the input files are of comparable lengths. To ensure this, we sort the

original file based on sequence length before splitting it into smaller chunks.

(2) *All work units should roughly involve the same amount of computation.* This needs to be ensured for efficient task distribution. The amount of computation depends on the total number of residues in the input files. This number has been parameterized as the lfactor, and can be specified as an input to the work generation process.

(3) *The size of the input data files should be optimized such that the amount of computation should be sufficient to justify the data communication overhead.* This can be done by adjusting the lfactor parameter mentioned above. A higher lfactor reduces the number of tasks and increases the computation time per task, and therefore leads to greater efficiency.

Keeping the above considerations in mind, the problem dataset, consisting of all the protein sequences of a set of genomes concatenated into a single file, is split into a number of smaller datasets, such that each smaller dataset has $lfactor$ number of residues. Given k such small datasets, $k = \lceil \frac{Total number of residues}{lfactor} \rceil$, each dataset needs to be compared to itself and every other dataset. Therefore, there are $k(k + 1)/2$ number of total comparisons. Since each workunit involves one such comparison, the work-generator daemon creates $k \cdot (k + 1)/2$ workunits in a steady stream. Once a host returns back a result, the SW scores are converted into E-values

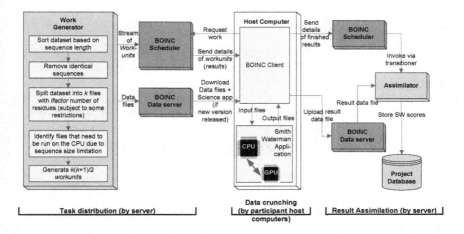

Figure 1.   Mapping of all-against-all genome comparison onto our grid architecture.

and stored in the project database. Figure 1 shows all steps involved in mapping all-against-all comparison onto the hybrid grid architecture.

3.2. *Data Parallelization on a GPU*

Given two sequences S_1 and S_2 of length l_1 and l_2, the Smith Waterman (SW) algorithm[15] computes their similarity $H(i, j)$ ending at position i and j in S_1 and S_2 respectively using the following recurrence relations for the affine gap penalty:

$$H(i, j) = \max(0, E(i, j), F(i, j), H(i - 1, j - 1) + sbt(S_1[i], S_2[j]))$$
$$E(i, j) = \max(H(i, j - 1) - \alpha, E(i, j - 1) - \beta) \tag{1}$$
$$F(i, j) = \max(H(i - 1, j) - \alpha, F(i - 1, j) - \beta) \tag{2}$$

where $sbt(i, j)$ is the substitution matrix, α is the gap penalty for the first gap and β is the gap penalty for subsequent gaps.

In order to map the SW algorithm efficiently mapped onto the GPU architecture, we take advantage of the fact that all elements in the same anti-diagonal of the DP matrix can be computed independent of each other in parallel. Therefore, parallelizing the algorithm involves computing the DP matrix in an anti-diagonal order. The anti-diagonals are stored as textures in the texture memory. Fragment programs are used to implement the arithmetic operations specified by the recurrence relation. The details can be found in Ref. 11.

3.3. *CPU Computation*

Although, the sequential CPU is less efficient than the GPU for our application, it is still essential to use CPU computation in our architecture. This is because:

- The length of query sequences is restricted by the size of the texture buffer. For example, On Geforce 6 and 7 series cards the length restriction is 4096. Thus, query sequences of length greater than 4096 must be run on the CPU.
- Dual or Multiple Core CPUs can increase the performance of parallel computation on CPU side. If there are additional free CPU resource during the GPU computation, we also use these resources for all-against-all comparisons. The corresponding framework is discussed in detail in Ref. 9

4. Performance Evaluation

In first experiment we want to measure the efficiency of the hybrid solution compared to standalone CPU comparison. We compared the runtimes for executing an all-against-all genome comparison among the following 6 microbial genomes: *Escherichia coli K12-MG1655, Bacillus anthracis Sterne, Mycobacterium avium paratuberculosis, Vibrio cholerae el tor n16961, Yersinia pestis KIM* and *Salmonella typhimurium LT2 SGSC1412*. The dataset consists of 26, 409 gene sequences. The maximum and average sequence lengths are 6384 and 311. The dedicated system uses a standalone CPU (Intel Pentium 4, 3GHz, 1GB RAM running Windows XP) and a standalone NVIDIA GeForce 7800 GTX. This comparison was performed using FASTA OSEARCH[14] on the standalone CPU and our hybrid code. The GPU computing uses the high-level GPU programming language GLSL. The runtimes for the dedicated system are shown in Table 1. It can be seen that because of the batch processing, the GPU is able to accelerate large-scale sequence comparison tasks based on the Smith-Waterman algorithm by one order of magnitude.

Table 1. Performance comparison between a single dedicated CPU and GPU.

	CPU	GPU
Runtime (mins)	14938.30	2208.90
Speedup	–	6.76

In the second experiment we evaluate the efficiency of the grid architecture. We have set up a BOINC project with BOINC server version 5.2.8 on an Intel Pentium 4, 3.00 GHz server running Fedora Core 4 Linux with an Apache 2.0 web server. To benchmark the performance of our hybrid computing model, we have set up a campus-wide GPU-accelerated BOINC desktop grid with the following configuration of host computers:

We use the same dataset as in Experiment 1 to measure the efficiency of the GPU grid. Table 3 shows the runtime comparison on our grid testbed for a varying number of clients. We have used a value of $lfactor = 500,000$ (the approximate number of residues per input file - see Section 3.1) for this comparison. It can be seen that the speedup of the grid testbed is almost the same as the incremental number of clients. On 2 and 4 clients, the efficiency of grid architecture is higher than dedicated 7800GTX, this can be explained that GPU of 7900GTX has higher performance than the the GPU of 7800GTX. It also can be observed that the efficiency drops

Table 2. Hardware configuration of our GPU grid.

Quantity	CPU configuration:
8	Intel Pentium 4, 3.00GHz CPU 1GB RAM running Windows XP with BOINC client version 5.4.11
Quantity	GPU configurations:
4	NVIDIA GeForce 7900 GTX 622 MHz engine clock speed, 1.83 GHz memory clock speed,
2	NVIDIA GeForce 7950 GT 600 MHz engine clock speed, 1.45 MHz memory clock speed,
1	NVIDIA GeForce 7800 GTX 550 MHz engine clock speed, 1.7 GHz memory clock speed,
1	NVIDIA GeForce 6800 GTX 370 MHz engine clock speed, 1 GHz memory clock speed,

with an increasing number of clients. This can be explained by lower host availability for an increasing number of hosts.

Table 3. Performance on our GPU-accelerated BOINC testbed for a varying number of clients.

Clients Number	2	4	6	8
Runtime (mins)	886	517	424	336
Efficiency compared to one 7800GTX	249.3%	427.3%	521.0%	657.4%
Efficiency compared to same number of 7800GTX	124.6%	106.8%	82.8%	82.2%

5. Comparative Genomics Study Using Possession of tRNA Substrate

Bacterial tRNA Adenosine Deaminase activity is highly specific for its substrate, a single arginine decoding tRNA. The gene and primary transcript of this tRNA has an adenosine at the anti-codon *wobble* position which must be deaminated to inosine in order for the tRNA function productively in translation of mRNA to proteins. Inspection of microbial tRNA distributions as predicted from whole genome sequences reveals that some microbes have the appropriate adenosine deaminase substrate while others do not.[16] We can regard possession of the tRNA substrate as a molecular phenotype, and therefore classify the substrate positive microbes as phenotype positive and the substrate negative microbes conversely, inferring that the phenotype positive set must genetically encode the functional capacity to convert the wobble adenosine to inosine.

Thus, the requirements for a genotype to phenotype analysis are met in this case, and we can proceed to assemble the data as an input to PheGee.

Table 4. The selected phenotype positive/negative genomes.

Microbial Genome Name	TIGR Genome Reference	Encodes tRNA substrate for tRNA Adenosine Deaminase (+/-)
Escherichia coli K12	Escherichia coli K12-MG1655	+
Bacillus subtilis	Bacillus subtilis 168	+
Haemophilus influenzae	Haemophilus influenzae 86 028NP	+
Vibrio cholerae	v_cholerae_el_tor_n16961	+
Mycobacterium tuberculosis	M. tuberculosis H37Rv (lab strain)	+
Staphylococcus aureus	Staphylococcus aureus N315	+
Buchnera aphidicola	Buchnera aphidicola Sg	+
Bartonella henselae	Bartonella henselae Houston-1	+
Caulobacter crescentus	C_crescentus_cb15	+
Chlamydia trachomatis	Chlamydia trachomatis serovar D	+
Mycoplasma pneumoniae	Mycoplasma pneumoniae M129	-
Borrelia burgdorferi	b_burgdorferi_b31	-
Campylobacter jejuni	c_jejuni_rm1221	-
Helicobacter pylori	h_pylori_26695	-
Mycoplasma genitalium	m_genitalium_g_37	-
Pyrococcus furiosus	Pyrococcus furiosus DSM 3638	-
Methanococcus jannaschii	m_jannaschii_dsm2661	-
Archaeoglobus fulgidus	a_fulgidus_dsm4304	-
Thermotoga maritima	t_maritima_msb8	-
Sulfolobus tokodaii	Sulfolobus tokodaii strain 7	-

We first selected a corresponding set of ten phenotype positive microbial genomes ($\pi+$) and ten phenotype negative microbial genomes ($\pi-$), which is shown in Table 4. The compilation of tRNA sequences and sequences of tRNA genes from http://www.tRNA.uni-bayreuth.de[16] was used to classify each genome. The complete set of annotated protein sequences from each genome was obtained from TIGR (www.tigr.org). We then performed an all-against-all comparison on our grid testbed as described in Section 3. The results were input to PheGee, which then reported 163 genes to have the highest partitioning score in $\pi+$. We further analyzed these genes for clusters of homologues. This was done by constructing a graph $G = (V, E)$ where V is the set of 163 genes and

$$E = \{(g_{i,k}, g_{j,l}) : \arg\min_{1 \le x \le \phi(j)} d(g_{i,k}, g_{j,l}) = l\}$$

G was then searched for cliques of maximal size.

We further ranked the cliques by their average E-value distance to the top hits in the phenotype negative sets. Thus, a set of yfhC homologues genes is identified as the most of significant clique (see Table 5[a]). The bacterial tRNA adenosine deaminase has been actually biochemically characterized in E. coli.[18] The enzyme is encoded by the tadA gene (called yfhC

---

[a]Shorten Table to only show Clique #1.

prior to experimental functional attribution). PheGee is able to discover a cluster of homologous genes in the phenotype positive set that includes tadA (yfhC) from E.coli. Thus, we are able infer the gene responsible for an enzymatic activity from the phylogenetic distribution of the enzyme substrate.

Table 5. The identified clique with the highest average distance score in $\pi+$ and corresponding genes (TIGR reference numer) in each phenotype positive genome.

	Clique #1 (yfhC)
Avg. Distance	2.24
E. coli K12	b2559, putative deaminase (yfhC)
Vibrio cholerae	VC0864, zinc-binding domain protein (yfhC)
Bacillus subtilis	Bsu0018, similar to hypothetical proteins (yaaJ)
Haemo. influenzae	NTHI1073, conserved hypothetical protein
M.tuberculosis	Rv3752c, hypothetical protein Rv3752c
Buchner.	BUsg246, hypothetical 20.0 kD protein in purL-dpj (yfhC)
Bartonella henselae	BH02600, Nitrogen fixation protein
Chlam. trachomatis	CT844, cytosine deaminase (yfhC)
Caulob. crescentus	CC0231, cytidine and deoxycytidylate deaminase family protein
Staphyloc. aureus	SA0516, hypothetical protein, similar to Cu binding protein

6. Conclusion

In this paper, we have introduced a new computational grid architecture based on a hybrid computing model. The architecture consists of two types of parallelism: (1) a desktop grid for coarse-grained parallelization; and (2) GPUs for fine-grained parallelization. We have shown how a comparative genomics application can be efficiently mapped onto this type of architecture and biologically validated the produced results using a new phenotype-genotype exploration method. Our implementation achieves significant speedups on our grid prototype, which consists of easily programmable mass-produced graphics hardware available for less than US$400 at any local computer outlet. This direction even provides a zero-cost solution for labs with access to desktops with modern graphics cards. The very rapid growth of genomic databases demands even more powerful high performance solutions in the near future. Hence, our results are especially encouraging since GPU performance grows faster than Moore's law as it applies to CPUs.

References

1. Genomes online database. www.genomesonline.org. updated on October 30, 2006.
2. *BOINC: a system for public-resource computing and storage*, 2004.

3. S.F. Altschul, W. Gish, W. Miller, E.W Myers, and D.J. Lipman. Basic local alignment search tool. *J. Mol. Biol.*, 215:403–410, 1990.

4. David P. Anderson, Jeff Cobb, Eric Korpela, Matt Lebofsky, and Dan Werthimer. Seti@home: an experiment in public-resource computing. *Communications of the ACM*, 45(11):56–61, November 2002.

5. S. Brenner, C. Chothia, and T. Hubbard. Assessing sequence comparison methods with reliable structurally identified distant evolutionary relationships. *Biochemistry*, 95(11):6073–6078, 1998.

6. Claire M. Fraser, Jonathan Eisen, Robert D. Fleischmann, Karen A. Ketchum, and Scott Peterson. Comparative genomics and understanding of microbial biology. *Emerging Infectious Diseases*, 6(5):505–512, 2000.

7. Masumi Itoh, Tatsuya Akutsu, and Minoru Kanehisa. Clustering of database sequences for fast homology search using upper bounds on alignment score. *Genome Informatic*, 15(1):93–104, 2004.

8. Masumi Itoh, Susumu Goto, Tatsuya Akutsu, and Minoru Kanehisa. Fast and accurate database homology search using upper bounds of local alignment scores. *Bioinformatics*, 21(7):912–921, 2005.

9. Weiguo Liu, Qi Liu, Bertil Schmidt, Chen Chen, Gerrit Voss, Alexei Sourin, and Wolfgang Müller-Wittig. A cpu-gpu collaborative architecture for parallel desktop computing. In *EuroPar 2007*, submitted to.

10. Weiguo Liu, Bertil Schmidt, Gerrit Voss, and Wolfgang Müller-Wittig. GPU-ClustalW: Using graphics hardware to accelerate multiple sequence alignment. In *Proc. High Performance Computing 2006*, pages 363–374, 2006.

11. Weiguo Liu, Bertil Schmidt, Gerrit Voss, and Wolfgang Müller-Wittig. Streaming algorithms for biological sequence alignment on GPUs. *IEEE Transaction on Parallel and Distributed Systems*, to appear.

12. D Manocha. General purpose computations using graphics processors. *IEEE Computer*, 20(7):85–88, 2005.

13. John D. Owens, David Luebke, Naga Govindaraju, Mark Harris, Jens Krüger, Aaron E. Lefohn, and Timothy J. Purcell. A survey of general-purpose computation on graphics hardware. In *Proc. Eurographics 2005, State of the Art Reports*, pages 21–51, 2005.

14. W. R. Pearson. Flexible sequence similarity searching with the FASTA3 program package. *Methods Mol. Biol.*, 132:185–219, 2000.

15. T. F. Smith and M. S. Waterman. Identification of common molecular subsequences. *J. Mol. Biol.*, 147(1):195–197, March 1981.

16. M. Sprinzl and K.S. Vassilenko. Compilation of tRNA sequences and sequences of tRNA genes. *Nucleic Acids Research*, 33:139–140, January 2005.

17. Michela Taufer, Chahm An, Andreas Kerstens, and Charles L. Brooks III. Predictor@Home: Protein Structure Prediction Supercomputer Based on Global Computing. *IEEE Transactions on Parallel and Distributed Computing*, 17(8):786–796, 2006.

18. J. Wolf, A.P. Gerber, and W. Keller. tada, an essential tRNA-specific adenosine deaminase from Escherichia coli. *The EMBO Journal*, 21:3841–3851, 2002.

DIGITAL MEDIA PORTAL FOR THE GRID

BU-SUNG LEE, MING TANG and JUNWEI ZHANG

School of Computer Engineering
Nanyang Technological University, Singapore 639798
{ebslee, tangm, jwzhang}@ntu.edu.sg

The Grid portal provides an environment where the user can access Grid resources, execute and monitor Grid jobs, and collaborate with other users. This paper reports on the development of the digital media Grid portal specifically to meet the needs of the media Grid community, which supports digital media processing, delivery, and storage in the Grid. The architecture of the media Grid portal and the solutions for system performance optimization and fault-tolerance are described in detail.

1. Introduction

Over the past decade the growth of the Grid technology has been exponential. It is considered as the next wave to follow the WWW. One of the major issue that has been addressed by the Grid research communities is the ease of access. To reach out to the general users, it is essential to build the Grid portals. The portal provides a web-based authentication and access to the Grid resources. Many generic portals have been developed for general use, where users can upload their data for process. A number of Grid portal framework, e.g., JetSpeed and OGCE, have been applied to modularize the development of portal service.

The digital media portal is a point of access to the Grid environment to carry out the computing tasks for various media. Through the media portal, the user can access Grid resources, execute and monitor Grid jobs, and collaborate with other users on the media rich work.

In this research, we build a media rich portal specifically to meet the needs of the media Grid community. The media portal aims to support digital media processing, delivery, and storage. The media could be in the forms of audio, video, image, animation and graphics. Currently the portal system can support multiple digital media applications successfully, such as Pixie, Mental Ray, POV-Ray and interactive rendering. A novel character of our portal is that it provides both interfaces to the conventional web browser and the commercial graphics software, Maya. Thus, the animators can submit rendering jobs either from web browser or from Maya on their desktop PC to the Grid directly. The digital media processing results are displayed dynamically to the end-user through the portal, and the user can monitor and manage the Grid jobs.

Running digital media application in the large-scale Grid environment is much more complicated than in a single computer or a rendering farm. In particular, the system performance optimization and fault-tolerance become prominent issues as the Grid is a dynamically changing environment. According to our experiments, the Network File System (NFS), which is widely used in computer clusters, will be a serious bottleneck when a number of processes read and write on the same NFS disk. A practical method is provided to solve the NFS bottleneck problem by making the Grid jobs run on local disks only. This method is clearly described in the wrapper program for the Pixie application. On the other hand, the failure events such as job missing and data transfer error occur frequently. Solutions to recover the failures are given.

The rest of the paper is organized as follows. Section 2 discusses the Grid portal related works. Section 3 presents the architecture of the digital media Grid portal. The Pixie rendering and some other digital media applications that are adapted to the Grid environment are introduced. The issues and solutions on the system performance optimization and fault-tolerance are given in Section 4. Section 5 concludes this paper.

2. Related Work

The Grid portal is defined as a problem solving environment that allows users to access and execute Grid applications from a conventional Web browser.[4] The Grid portals are classified into science portals and user portals. The science portals are also called application portals and they allow the scientist to focus completely on the science problem at hand by making the Grid a transparent extension of their desktop computing environment. The user portals provide the user with direct views of Grid resources and services, and they require the user to have a deeper understanding of Grid technology. The user portals provide Grid services such as single sign-on, job submission and status tracking.

Grid Portal Toolkit (GridPort)[6] is a Perl solution for building Grid Portals, and it uses the Globus toolkit to access remote resources for job execution and information services. GridPort provides a collection of services, scripts and tools that allow developers to connect Web-based interfaces to the computational Grid.

Grid Portal Development Kit (GPDK),[5] which was produced as part of the USA Department of Energy (DOE) Science Grid project, packaged a template portal and a collection of tools and several key reuseable service components that allowed developers to rapidly construct customized portals. GPDK is a Java based implementation built on top of the Java CoG,[19] which provides the core Java technology to access the foundational Grid services.

The Open Grid Computing Environment (OGCE)[10] is a project funded by US National Science Foundation to provide sharable Grid portal solutions by leveraging a number of ongoing portal development efforts.

3. Media Grid Portal Architecture

The architecture of the media Grid portal is shown in Figure 1. The media portal builds upon the uPortal portal framework.[18] uPortal is a widely used portal framework in academic communities, and it is JSR 168[7] compliant.

A core set of JSR 168 compatible Grid portlets provided by OGCE Release 2 are deployed, including GridFTP file transfer, GSI proxy management, and job submission. To support various digital media applications to run in the Grid environment, different portlets have been developed and deployed for them. Specifically, the portlets for Pixie, Mental Ray, POV-Ray and interactive modeler are created, and the details of these applications will be discussed in the following section. The digital media applications are installed in the computer clusters in the Grid. To enable the media applications run in the Grid environment and automate the job management, these applications are wrapped with programming scripts, which execute the complicated and miscellaneous functions, such as execution environment setup, input data fetching, input data pre-processing, data decompression, job execution, resultant data transmission, and execution environment cleanup. Properly wrapping the Grid applications with scripts can significantly simplify the job submission and management in the Grid environment. A specific wrapped Grid application will be given in section 3.2.

3.1. *Meta-Scheduler*

The meta-scheduler resides on top of the local job schedulers, which manage computational resources for individual computer clusters and high performance computers. The meta-scheduler efficiently coordinates computing resource management across the collection of computer clusters. The meta-scheduler provides central job and resource management, enabling users to submit jobs without requiring knowledge of the Grid configuration and status. When users submit jobs to the meta-scheduler, the meta-scheduler coordinates with all local schedulers to understand current system status, and then makes scheduling decisions. The major functions provided by the meta-scheduler are job submission, job monitoring, and data transfer control.

Our digital media portal can be integrated with any available meta-scheduler, and the major changes are on the interface with the meta-scheduler when submitting and managing the Grid jobs. For current implementation of our system, LSF, which stands for Load Sharing Facility from Platform Computing Corporation, is used as the meta-scheduler for the Grid. LSF is a general purpose distributed queuing system that is able to unite a number of computer clusters or hosts into a single virtual system to make better use of the resources on a network.[1] Hosts from various vendors can be integrated into a seamless system, where LSF can find the best host to run the programs. LSF can automatically select hosts in a heterogeneous environment based on the current load conditions and the resource requirements of the applications. LSF uses First-Come First-Serve (FCFS) scheduling policy, and the jobs are dispatched based on their order in the queue.

As shown in Figure 1, there are three computer clusters in the system: *melon*, *hpc-pdpm* and *guava*. Clusters *melon* and *hpc-pdpm* both have 20 CPUs, and *guava* has 10 CPUs. Clusters *melon* and *guava* are located in National Grid Office (NGO) of Singapore, and *hpc-pdpm* is in Nanyang Technological University (NTU) of Singapore. All of these three clusters run with Sun Grid Engine (SGE) local resource scheduler.[14] Thus, after a job is dispatched to a computer cluster by LSF meta-scheduler, SGE on this cluster will take charge of the job consequently. And the job will be scheduled by SGE and run on the nodes of the cluster.

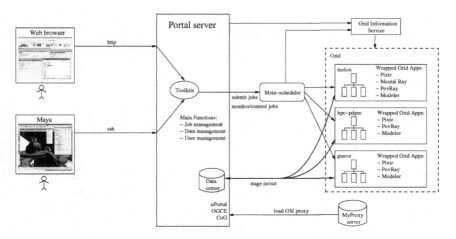

Figure 1.   System architecture of the digital media portal for the Grid.

3.2. *Pixie Rendering Application*

RenderMan[13] is a technical specification for interfacing between modeling and rendering programs. The RenderMan interface standard is defined by Pixar.[11] RenderMan Interface Bytestream (RIB) is an ASCII or binary metafile format, and it encodes a sequence of RenderMan API calls. The RenderMan API is a collection of functions that are used by an application to transfer geometry and rendering attributes to the renderer and to control the rendering process. RIB file is used to pass scene information (model data, lights, camera, shaders, attributes, and options) to a RenderMan renderer to control image that it will render. RIB file is useful for archival and later rendering, and rendering over a network.

As shown in Figure 2, RenderMan is used to make the procedural API calls for the modeler. For each RenderMan API call, the modeler program outputs the corresponding RIB to a file. The archival RIB can later be sent to a standalone renderer, which inputs the RIB and outputs rendered images.

Pixie[12] renderer is a RenderMan compliant photo-realistic rendering toolkit. Pixie is capable of producing motion-picture-quality output and implements all RenderMan 3.2 primitives, such as quadrics, parametrics, subdivision surfaces, points, curves and convex/concave polygons. It also provides the functions of high quality texture/shadow, raytracing, motion blur, global illumination, etc.

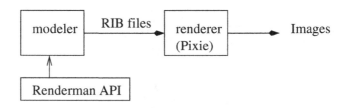

Figure 2.   Procedures of modeling and rendering with RenderMan.

Maya[2] is the one of the most popular and powerful 3D modeling and animation software, and it is used by artists to make 3D models and animations. Many of the world's leading films, TV programs, and commercial advertisements are from Maya created 3D animations. Although Maya also provides 3D rendering solutions, the highly cost rendering farm is not affordable and cost-effective for most of the small rendering industries. To translate Maya to RenderMan and use the open source Pixie for rendering will be a better solution, especially when the Grid resources are available.

As a translator from Maya to RenderMan, Liquid[8] is an open source plugin for the Maya 3D animation package, and it allows the animator to output any Render-Man compatible renderers. By installing Liquid plugin in Maya, the animator can convert the editing Maya model into RenderMan RIB files. The output RIB files can be compressed into a ZIP package, which also include the necessary textures and shaders. Then the animator can upload the ZIP package to the portal using the Web browser and submit the rendering jobs to the Grid. The user can monitor the job status and preview the resultant images from the portal. After all frames are done, the user can download the packaged resultant images that are stored in the data server.

It is required to provide a friendly and familiar interface to the animators for job submission in the Grid environment. It will be desirable to hide the back-end details of the Grid environment, and allow the animators to keep their current working environment. It will be more attractive if the Grid portal also provides interfaces to the commercial graphics software, e.g. Maya, to facilitate the rendering job submission to the Grid.

As the plugin to Maya is programmable, the rendering job submission can be done from Maya to the portal server directly. And the portal server will manage the rendering jobs. The steps to submit a job through Maya to the Grid are:

(1) After editing the graphics in Maya, the animator submits the rendering jobs by simply clicking a plugin menu buttons. The animator can specify the frames to be rendered. After submission, the user can shutdown the graphics software at anytime.
(2) Maya software calls a local script that remotely invokes the job submission command provided by the portal server.
(3) The portal server submits the rendering jobs to LSF, and the data stage in /stage out will be carried out between the portal server and the LSF submission host automatically.
(4) When the animator wants to check the job status, he can login to the Web page provided by the portal server. From the Web page, user can get the information such as completion percentages, job running time, and resultant images with different resolutions.
(5) After the rendering jobs are done, the animator can collect the output data from the data storage.

We have developed the portlets that supports Pixie rendering, which have been integrated into the media Grid portal. The portlets of Pixie job submission, job monitoring and resultant image preview are shown in Figure 3. For Pixie application, each Pixie rendering job will process one RIB file, which is associated with one frame in the animation. The user can submit a batch of jobs to processes the frames from the animation. Then the portal submits the batch of Pixie rendering jobs to the meta-scheduler. The job management function provided by the portal is based on the job batch.

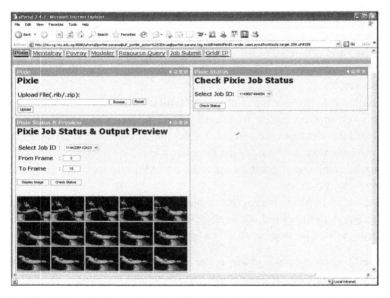

Figure 3.   The Pixie rendering portlets, including job submission, status monitoring and output preview.

The meta-scheduler decides the job running sites by analyzing the requirements of the jobs and the status of the Grid system. The resultant rendering image (TIFF) files will be compressed and then transferred from the job running sites to the portal server automatically. The portal server dynamically displays the thumbnails of the rendered images to end users. After all image frames have been generated and transferred to the portal server, they will be compressed into one package so that the user can download it promptly.

3.3. Other Digital Media Applications

Besides the Pixie rendering application, Mental Ray, POV-Ray and interactive modeling are also supported by our system.

Mental Ray[3] is a production quality rendering application developed by Mental Images Inc.[9] The primary feature of mental ray is the achievement of high performance through parallelism on both multiprocessor machines and across render farms. The efficient support for multi-threaded and network rendering in mental ray is based on parallel rendering algorithms. Multi-threading takes advantage of multiple processors, hyper-threaded and multi-core processors available in a system, without requiring any additional licenses. Due to the job system distributing jobs to multiple threads, the performance of mental ray scales with the number of processors available. In our Grid environment, Mental Ray is installed in the *melon* cluster. Mental Ray has been integrated into Alias Maya[2] and other software. A number of translators and translator plug-ins allow for using Mental Ray in conjunction with various 3D modeling and animation front-end systems.

POV-Ray[16] is a ray tracing program available for a variety of computer platforms. Different from many other 3D computer modeling packages, which typically use triangle meshes to compose all objects, POV-Ray internally represents objects using mathematical definitions and all POV-Ray primitive objects can be described by mathematical functions. This fact provides POV-Ray with several advantages over other rendering/modeling systems. POV-Ray primitives are usually more accurate than their polygonal counterparts. Objects that can be described in terms of spheres, planar surfaces, cylinders, tori and the like are perfectly smooth and mathematically accurate in POV-Ray renderings, whereas polygonal artifacts may be visible in mesh-based modeling software. POV-Ray primitives are also simpler to define than most of their polygonal counterparts. The POV-Ray package includes detailed instructions on using the ray-tracer and creating scenes. Many stunning scenes are included with POV-Ray to creating images. These scenes can be modified so it is not necessary to start from scratch.

Interactive modeler allows free-form shape modeling for the models with function-based representation. The interactive modeling and rendering are achieved by using the Grid resources and Java3D technique.

4. Performance Optimization and Fault-Tolerance

In the Grid environment with large-scale of heterogeneous computational resources, running digital media applications is much more complicated than in a single computer. In particular, the application performance optimization and fault-tolerance become prominent issues in distributed systems. When a large number of jobs running in the Grid system, the performance bottleneck caused by the sharing resources must be avoid. Meanwhile, as the distributed system situation changes dynamically, some failures will happen frequently when running jobs in the Grid, which will be unacceptable to the end-users. Thus, fault-tolerance also takes an important role in order to successfully utilize the Grid resources to support computing intensive applications and satisfy the user requirements. In this section, we discuss the issues of performance optimization and fault-tolerance that are met when implementing the Grid enabled digital media applications, and the solutions for these issues are also provided.

Network File System (NFS) is a protocol originally developed by Sun Microsystems as a distributed file system which allows a computer to access files over a network as easily as if they were on its local disks. Most computer clusters are installed with NFS, so that all nodes in a cluster can easily access the shared data and software in NFS. On the other hand, NFS could be the bottleneck for the computer cluster especially when multiple processes reads and writes to the same disk partition over NFS. This becomes a problem since most implementations of NFS are known to be lackluster in performance, and perform synchronous write commands.

Besides, access to an NFS served disk is much slower than to a local disk. For example, it was reported in Ref. 17 that the elapsed runtimes can increase by a factor of up to five when a remote disk served via NFS is used compared to a local disk. The faster the machine, the greater the impact of the NFS-served disk bottleneck is. This is because NFS read and write rates of 500 kbytes/second over Ethernet are considered fairly good results, whereas fast SCSI disks run at 10Mbytes/second. Furthermore, unnecessary remote disk accesses load the network and impact other network users. Hence the amount of heavy data processing that occurs over NFS should be minimized. To use local disks can provide better performance and avoid to degrade the network performance.

We also met the NFS bottleneck issue when we executed digital media applications in the computer cluster. We did an experiment on cluster *hpc-pdpm*, which has ten nodes and 20 CPUs. When 20 Pixie rendering jobs run on the cluster and all the jobs read and write to the same NFS disk, the execution time of every job is more than five times slower than the execution time when only one Pixie job runs in the cluster. To avoid the NFS bottleneck problem, the jobs should read and write to local disks on the computers.

The techniques used in our research to improve the Pixie rendering performance in the Grid environment can be got from the Pixie wrapper $GridPixie$ shown in Figure 4.

Wrapper $GridPixie$ takes three arguments: the input RIB file (RIB), the ID of the batch jobs ($JobBatchID$), and the corresponding user ID ($UserID$). According to $JobBatchID$ and $UserID$, the wrapper can decide the job working directory and manage the input/ouput data automatically. To minimize the data transfer over WAN, the textures and shaders are transferred only once for every computer cluster. $NFSDir$ is the working directory for the job batch in the cur-

$GridPixie(RIB, JobBatchID, UserID)$

1: Let $NFSDir$ be the working directory for the job batch, and it is in the NFS of the current computer cluster.

2: **if** $NFSDir$ does not exist **then**

3:     Create directory $NFSDir$.

4:     Download all textures and shaders from portal server to $NFSDir$.

5: **else**

6:     Wait till the downloading is done.

7: **end if**

8: Let $LocalDir$ be the job execution directory in the local disk of the current computer node.

9: **if** $LocalDir$ does not exist **then**

10:     Create directory $LocalDir$.

11:     Copy all textures and shaders from $NFSDir$ to $LocalDir$.

12: **else**

13:     Wait till the copying is done.

14: **end if**

15: Download RIB file from the portal server to $LocalDir$.

16: cd $LocalDir$

17: Call Pixie render for RIB.

18: Upload the resultant TIFF file to the portal server.

19: Cleanup.

Figure 4. Wrapped Pixie application for the Grid.

rent computer cluster, and it is on NFS that can be accessed directly by all nodes in the cluster. The first incoming job of the batch to the computer cluster will create the directory of $NFSDir$ and download all textures and shaders from the portal server to $NFSDir$ (line 3 and line 4). The rest incoming jobs of the batch to the cluster can continue the next steps only if the textures and shaders have been downloaded completely by the first job to the cluster. $LocalDir$ is the execution directory in the local disk of the current computer node. The first incoming job of the batch to the computer node will create the directory of $LocalDir$ and copy all textures and shaders from $NFSDir$ to $LocalDir$ (line 10 and line 11). The rest incoming jobs of the batch to the node can start from line 15 only if all textures and shaders have been copied to $LocalDir$ by the first job to the node. After that, the wrapper downloads the RIB file from the portal server to $LocalDir$ (line 15), goes to $LocalDir$ (line 16), and calls the original Pixie rendering command (line 17). After the rendering is done, the wrapper uploads the resultant TIFF file to the portal server and cleans up the execution environment.

Failures are not unusual in the large-scale distributed systems. To satisfy the end-user's requirements, the failure events must be traced and the failure tasks should be recovered. Two kinds of failures occur frequently in the media Grid system: job missing and data transfer error. As afore said, our media portal is integrated LSF meta-scheduler, and the LSF meta-scheduler interacts with the local resource manager, SGE, which runs in every computer cluster. We find that sometimes several jobs are missing when hundreds of jobs are submitted to the Grid in a batch. The error may be caused by LSF or SGE. The phenomena of the job missing is, after a large number of jobs have been submitted to the Grid, the status of some jobs will be changed to "DONE" but in fact they never run. To solve this problem, we create a fault-tolerance program that runs in the same site as the meta-scheduler. Whenever a job batch is submitted to the Grid with our system, the program will be invoked to trace the status of the jobs in the batch dynamically. If it is found that any job's status has been changed into "DONE", but the job is not executed at all, the program will re-submit this job to the Grid. The program will terminate when all jobs in the batch have been executed in the Grid.

In our system, OpenSSH[15] is used for data transmission to ensure the data security. In our system, it is very common that tens of jobs running in the Grid, which download and upload to the portal server simultaneously. Data transmission may fail occasionally especially when the data server is overloaded by too many concurrent connections. Thus, the status of each data transmission needs to be traced. Once it is found that a data transmission is failed due to too many connections to the data server, the task of the data transmission will be restarted after a random time interval to avoid the high collisions with the other data connections. This step will be repeated until the data transmission is done successfully.

5. Conclusion

This paper describes a digital media portal for the Grid that allows users access to Grid resources easily and makes the large-scale distributed environment manageable and productive.

The architecture and functions of the Grid portal are presented in details. A novel character of the portal is that it provides both interfaces to the conventional Web-based browser and the commercial graphics software, Maya. In this way, the animators can submit rendering jobs from Maya on their desktop PC to the Grid directly. As one of the digital media applications deployed in our system, the Pixie rendering is introduced. In the large-scale distributed system, performance optimization and fault-tolerance are two critical issues that must be solved efficiently. We present the techniques to overcome the NFS bottleneck problem that is common in the computer cluster. For the fault-tolerance issue, the methods to solve the frequently occurred failures of job missing and data transfer error are introduced.

Acknowledgements

This research is a part of the Adaptive Enterprise at Singapore (AE@SG) project. We would like to acknowledge the efforts of all the participants of AE@SG from National Grid Office (NGO) of Singapore, Nanyang Technological University, Institute of High Performance Computing of Singapore, and Singapore Management University. Infocomm Development Authority (IDA) of Singapore and HP sponsor this AE@SG project. In particular, we thank Professor Tony C. K. Yun, Professor Alexei Sourin, Mr. Chong Soon Keong and Mr. Konstantin Levinski for their cooperation on the digital media applications.

References

1. *Running Jobs with Platform LSF*. Platform Computing Cooperation, 2004.
2. Autodesk Maya. http://www.autodesk.com/alias.
3. T. Driemeyer. *Rendering with mental ray*. Springer Wien New York, 2000.
4. D. Gannon, G. Fox, M. Pierce, B. Plale, G. von Laszewski, C. Severance, J. Hardin, J. Alameda, M. Thomas, and J. Boisseau. Grid portals: A scientist's access point for grid service. In *GGF Community Practice document, working draft 1*, Sep 2003.
5. Grid Portal Development Kit (GPDK). http://doesciencegrid.org/projects/GPDK/.
6. GridPort. https://gridport.npaci.edu/.
7. JSR 168: Portlet Specification. http://www.jcp.org/en/jsr/detail?id=168.
8. Liquid – Maya to RenderMan Translator. http://liquidmaya.sourceforge.net/.
9. Mental Images Inc. http://www.mentalimages.com/.
10. OGCE. Open Grid Computing Environment. http://www.ogce.org.
11. Pixar. http://www.pixar.com/.
12. Pixie Renderer. http://www.cs.berkeley.edu/ okan/ Pixie/pixie.htm.
13. RenderMan. http://www.renderman.org/.
14. Sun N1 Grid Engine. http://www.sun.com/software/gridware/.
15. The OpenSSH Project. http://www.openssh.com/.
16. The Persistence of Vision Raytracer (POV-Ray). http://www.povray.org/.
17. The Starlink Project. http://www.starlink.rl.ac.uk/.
18. uPortal. http://www.uportal.org/.
19. G. von Laszewski, I. Foster, J. Gawor, and P. Lane. A Java Commodity Grid Kit. *Concurrency and Computation: Practice and Experience*, 13(8–9):643–662, 2001. http:/www.cogkit.org/.

Poster Papers

EXPLORING THE PC GRID TECHNOLOGY FOR RESEARCH COMPUTATION — THE NUS EXPERIENCE

TAN CHEE CHIANG and WANG JUNHONG

Computer Centre, National University of Singapore

The PC grid initiative at NUS, which is better known as the Tera-scale Campus Grid (TCG@NUS), is the single largest PC grid on campus in the region with more than 1,400 PCs linked up today. The creation of multi TFLOPS (Trillions of Floating-point Operations per Second) of computing power to support large-scale research computation was done without additional investment on High Performance Computing (HPC) hardware, a unique feature of such grid computing implementation that will be shared in this paper. Details on the returns of investment and the results of some case studies will be presented to demonstrate the viability and the strategic value of PC grid computing as an alternative to the traditional HPC approach for research computing.

The PC grid technologies allow the PC grid infrastructure to be extended to include not just desktops but also servers and clusters to form a single pool of computation resources. It will be shown in this paper that PC grid technologies are well suited for building the high throughput computational grid. The paper will also explore the possibility of extending the campus based infrastructure beyond the organisation boundary.

1. Introduction

Like many large universities, the National University of Singapore (NUS) has thousands of PCs installed across campus. Most of these PCs are not heavily loaded all the time and that presents a great opportunity to harness those unused compute cycles through Grid computing and use them for something useful, such as research computation. In the research computing environment, the greatest benefit of Grid Computing is probably the ability to create new computing capability that is otherwise not available if each computer is used separately. The combined computing power of large number of computers allows researchers to solve larger computation problems within the acceptable timeframe. This paper will show how such new computing capability can be created with a PC Grid implementation at NUS.

2. PC Grid Computing

The idle cycle harvesting concept of the PCs is not new. In fact, the first development of such software system was initiated in 1988 at University of Wisconsin, the Condor project (http://www.cs.wisc.edu/condor/). The more widespread adoption in recent years was probably due partly to the following developments:

- The significantly more powerful PCs owned by individuals and organisations. In 1988, an Intel 286 processor has a speed of around 20 MHz. Most of the PCs today come with processor speed of more than 3 GHz (3000 MHz). Whatever compute cycles that can be harvested will be more useful now.
- The availability of affordable broadband connection to home PCs. In early 1990s, 9.6 kbit/s was the available bandwidth for dialup to the Internet. Today, multiple Mbit/s and always on broadband connection from home is pretty common in many parts of the World.
- The emergence of supported commercial PC Grid middleware. Support and reliability are some of the important factors considered when organisation adopts certain solution for production implementation.

According to a study by IBM and Taurus (Taxonomy of Actual Utilisation of Real UNIX and Windows Servers – GM13-0191-00), the average daytime utilisation of desktops is usually less than 10%, which drops to being negligible in the evening. Assuming that we have 1000 2.6GHz PCs and there is a way to gather about 90% of unused resources and channel them to perform useful computation, we will be able to create a virtual computer with 900 2.6GHz processors and generate 4680 GFLOPS (Billions of floating-point operations per second) of computing power. In practice, not all connected PCs will be available all the time. Even with the assumption that only half is available at any time, the amount of compute cycles that can be harnessed will still be very impressive.

3. References

In general, PC Grid implementation can be categorised into two types: one that harvests the idle compute cycles within an organisation and the other does it over the Internet.

There are quite a number of Internet based @Home projects initiated over the past years. Some of the well known ones include SETI@Home (http://setiathome.berkeley.edu/) and folding@Home (http://folding.stanford.edu/). Such projects are making use of large amount of computing resources harvested from home PCs to run large scale research computation that will enhance knowledge and benefit humanity.

There are also universities, financial and pharmaceutical companies that have implemented similar PC Grid technologies within the organisation. Universities with large scale implementation include University of Texas at Austin, University of Florida and Purdue University. The difference between the intra-organisation implementation and the Internet based @HOME implementation is mainly in the reliability and efficiency of the resources harnessed. Usually the intra-organisation PCs are better maintained and likely to come with better network connection, hence more productive.

4. Implementation at NUS

The PC Grid implementation at NUS, more commonly known as Tera-scale Campus Grid or TCG@NUS, has been in operation since early 2005 with more than 1400 Windows based desktops and Linux systems. The resources are contributed by more than ten departments across campus, demonstrating fantastic spirit of sharing.

A commercial solution called Grid MP from United Devices has been deployed for the initiative. As shown in Figure 1, the solution consists of three primary components: Grid MP tools and interfaces (Application services), Grid MP Server and the Grid MP Agent.

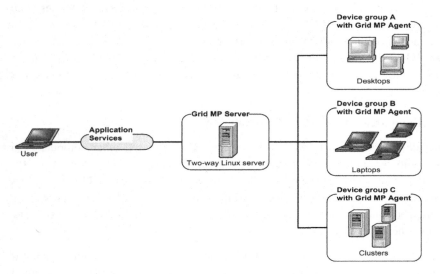

Figure 1: PC Grid at NUS.

The Grid MP tools and interfaces provide a variety of ways for users and applications to access and interact with the grid. The Grid MP Server optimises the resource utilisation by scheduling job requests to suitable underutilised resources based on constraints and policies such as job requirements, resource capability, resource availability and impact to the network. The primary function of the Grid MP Agent is to detect idle or underutilised CPU cycles on its computer, request jobs from Grid MP Server, execute jobs, and return results. PCs running the Grid MP Agent are organised into *device groups* for better management and control purposes.

The solution has addressed adequately two main concerns of the users and contributors on the use and sharing of such resources: Security and performance.

Security – All applications have to be digitally signed before they can be executed on the Grid. Data is encrypted during both network transmission and storage on compute nodes. Sandbox or a virtual runtime environment is created when a job is executing on a compute node. The sandbox ensures that the job behaves in a legitimate way on the compute node.

Performance – The solution ensures that the user's experience on the PC will not be affected in any way by having the PC forming part of the Grid. The solution also enables administrators to exert departmental control over their own resources with sophisticated policy engine.

Even though such PC grid technology is being used mainly to harness idle compute cycles from PCs, we find that the same technology will also work well when it is being implemented on server clusters. HPC servers usually have much higher utilisation level than PCs but they are still not 100% utilised all the time, and therefore it is still possible to harness significant amount of resources from them.

5. Comparison with Other Grid Solutions

Besides working on the PC Grid, we have also explored other compute Grid technologies such as those based on the open-source Globus ToolKits (GT). PC Grid is not a replacement for the conventional compute Grid but it does complement by creating a new capability from resources that are previously untapped. There are new learning points from our PC Grid implementation to be shared here.

Ease of deployment – A production PC Grid can be rolled out within a month if the PC clusters to be connected have been identified. Majority of the initial setting up time was being spent on the one-time installation and customisation of the Grid MP Server. Subsequently, it will take less than two minutes to add and get a new node ready for production use. In comparison, the GT based compute Grid we are working on is still evolving more than four years after we first started exploring in 2002.

Ease of administration & maintenance – The GT based implementation required the maintenance of local accounts on each site for remote execution of jobs. There is also a need to maintain a standard application software stack to enable portability and seamless execution. In the PC Grid model, both the application software and data are centrally managed on the Grid MP Server and forwarded to the compute node during run time. There is no need to set up a local account on the compute nodes. The only maintenance required on the compute nodes is the upgrade of the Grid MP Agent, which can be automated and done remotely without human intervention.

The PC grid we have implemented is basically a centrally managed infrastructure. Such model offers better security and the ease of administration and maintenance but offers less flexibility as compared to peer-to-peer model.

6. Return of Investment

Tangible return – The software investment of about US$180K allows connection of up to 3000 PCs. Using the same method used in section 2 to calculate the amount of resources that can be harvested, we will end up with an equivalent system with 1350 2.6GHz CPUs. A dedicated HPC cluster with that amount of computing power will probably cost more than US$2millions to install. Last year, a throughput of about 165,000 CPU hours was generated running one large scale bioinformatics application. Using the cost rating of US$1 per CPU hour as offered by one of the compute utility service providers, the investment can be recovered in less than two months.

Intangible return – Using each PC individually limits the size of the problem to be solved. Combining the compute powers of PCs and enabling them to be used as a single large computer allows researchers to attempt much larger computation and solving more challenging problems. The availability of such capability will help to enhance the competitiveness in computation based research. This is a case where the whole is greater than the sum.

7. Case Studies

Here are some case studies to demonstrate how the potential value of the PC Grid can be actualised. Some of these case studies were done when there were less than 1000 PCs connected.

	Software used	Problem definition	Results
Case study 1	tblastx	*Protein level sequence matching* • 22K sequences have to be searched against 3,461,799 sequences • Estimated to take about a month to complete on a 16-CPU server.	Took 20.5 hrs compute time on TCG, and 13 hrs reassembly times on a standalone PC. → About 21 times speedup compared to the 16-CPU server and about 336 times speedup with reference to a single CPU.
Case study 2	Autodock	*Virtual screening of chemical compounds for cancer research* • 80,000 chemical compounds from Chembridge and Chemdiv libraries are screened to identify candidates that can potentially inhibit the Mdm2/p53 interaction. • The problem size was determined to be impractical to run on a dedicated HPC cluster with 64 CPUs.	Within one month of running the jobs, more than 165,000 CPU-hours were consumed, completing more than 50% of the problem. → Generated about 3 times more CPU hours than the dedicated HPC clusters with more than 150 CPUs during the same period.
Case study 3	Modeler	*Comparative Modeling of Protein Structures* • Run 9999 jobs consisting of protein sequences with about 200 amino acid residues. • Took 42 days to complete on a 600MHz PC.	Took about 3 days to complete on TCG using around 100 PCs. → Reduce the compute time by about 39 days with a speedup of 14 times.
Case study 4	POV-Ray	*Image Rendering/Processing* • Render a 1024x768 pixel image by Mark Slone. • Took one day and 20 hours to complete on a Dell 3GHz PC.	Took about 100 minutes to complete on TCG with around 100 PCs. → Speed up of around 26 times. Impact will be greater if more images are rendered.
Case Study 5	User written application	*Decision Science – study of typical queue with Markov Chains model* • One run with moderate accuracy and parameter selection frequency took more than ten days to complete on a desktop.	On the TCG, it took just a few hours to complete one run with higher accuracy and parameter selection frequency. → More than 200 times speedup had been achieved

The above case studies show that the PC grid is well suited for data parallel application (Case study 1, 2, 3 and 4) and parametric study type of application (Case study 5).

8. A Platform for Sharing and Collaboration

It has been shown that the value of the PC Grid increases more than linearly with the increase of its size. It provides not just more resources but new capability to solve larger problem previously not possible on the non grid-enabled resources. To realise the maximum potential of the PC Grid, it has to be expanded beyond the organisation boundary. With the existing high-speed network interconnection and large number of PCs on various IHLs campuses, there is an opportunity to build a large wide-area campus grid. The following approaches are proposed for the possible collaboration:

Approach 1 - This approach is proposed to enable quick start of the possible collaboration. Researchers from other IHLs are invited to establish collaboration arrangement with researchers at NUS. Once a collaboration agreement is established, external collaborators will be given remote access to TCG@NUS. There will be no investment required in this approach as shown in Figure 2. External collaborators can also use the TCG@NUS as a testbed for evaluation purposes.

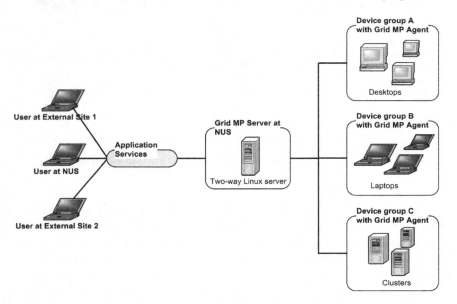

Figure 2: Remote access to TCG@NUS.

188

Approach 2 – The 2nd approach will be considered when the collaborating IHLs are ready to invest and share but do not wish to build and operate their own grid. The interested IHL can just purchase the Grid MP Agent licenses and continue to share the Grid MP Server at NUS. In this model, a decentralised control is created through the device group administrator accounts. The owners of the PCs outside of NUS will retain control over their resources. In this approach and the previous approach, researchers will be able to use application software we have Grid-enabled on our Grid MP Server. The implementation will be easy and cost effective as only the Grid MP Agent will be added.

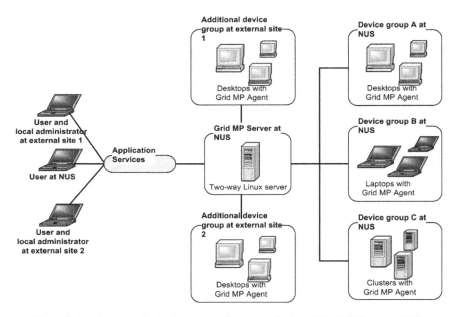

Figure 3: Resource contribution from external sites and sharing of Grid MP Server at NUS.

Approach 3 - When the other collaborating IHLs are ready to build their own PC Grid, each site can then has its own full-fledged PC Grid infrastructure on campus. Another Grid middleware can then be used to enable sharing between each site. In this case, the PC Grid solution deployed at each site needs not be the same. A meta-scheduler solution that allows resource sharing between different types of grids can be implemented to enable the sharing.

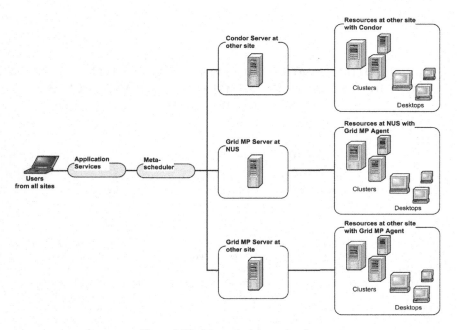

Figure 4: The Meta-scheduler approach.

9. Conclusion

It has been proven at NUS that PC Grid has matured to the extent where it can significantly augment existing HPC technologies in advancing research computation. It has also been shown that the value (the intangible returns) of the PC Grid increases exponentially as its size increases. It means that the PC Grid will have to expand beyond its campus boundary in order to achieve greater value and capability. NUS is open to working with any IHLs that are interested to share such PC grid resources.

References

Grid – A Low Cost, High Speed Alternative to Traditional High Performance Computing - http://www.ud.com/resources/files/wp_grid_roi.pdf.

PC Grid Computing at NUS -
http://www.nus.edu.sg/comcen/svu/pcgrid/about_PCGrid.html

United Devices' Grid MP on Intel Architecture -
http://www.ud.com/resources/files/wp_intel_ud.pdf

GRID COMPUTING FOR STOCHASTIC
SUPER-RESOLUTION IMAGING: FUNDAMENTALS
AND ALGORITHMS

JING TIAN and KAI-KUANG MA

School of Electrical and Electronic Engineering,
Nanyang Technological University, Singapore 639798
Email: jingtian@ieee.org, ekkma@ntu.edu.sg

The *super-resolution* (SR) imaging refers to the image processing algorithms for overcoming the inherent limitations of the image acquisition systems to produce high-resolution images from their low-resolution counterparts. In our recent work, a stochastic SR imaging framework has been successfully developed by applying the *Markov chain Monte Carlo* (MCMC) technique and shown as a promising approach for addressing the SR problem. To further overcome the intensive computation requirement of the stochastic SR imaging, Grid computing is resorted in this paper to break down the computationally-intensive MCMC SR task into a set of independent and small sub-tasks for parallel computing in the Grid computing environment. Experiments are conducted to show that Grid computing can effectively accelerating the execution time of the stochastic SR algorithm.

1. Introduction

The goal of *super-resolution* (SR) imaging is to obtain an image with a higher resolution from low-resolution observations directly afforded by the physical image acquisition sensors [1, 2]. Naturally, there is always a high demand for high-resolution images, for they enable users to see more image details, which are difficult or impossible to detect in the low-resolution observations. For that, the SR imaging technique provides an effective and inexpensive software approach, as demonstrated in Figure 1.

Recently, a stochastic SR approach has been successfully proposed by exploiting the *Markov chain Monte Carlo* (MCMC) technique with attractive performance [2]. The developed stochastic SR approach requires substantial amounts of computational resources, for it not only needs to generate a huge number of samples, but also requires exhaustive searches for determining the optimal model parameters.

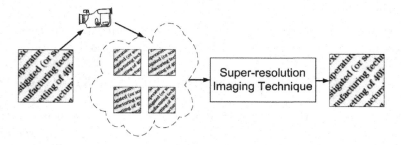

Figure 1. A conceptual framework of the super-resolution imaging.

Grid computing appears as a promising technology to handle the intensive computation challenge, for it can performs many independent computations at once using multiple computation processes, rather than doing these computations sequentially using a single computation process only [3–5].

In this paper, Grid computing is exploited to tackle the computationally intensive SR imaging problem. The complicated MCMC SR task is broke down into a number of independent sub-tasks. These independent sub-tasks are then dispatched to the Grid computing service for parallel computing. Finally, the respective results obtained from different sub-tasks are assembled to generate the final result for the entire MCMC SR task.

The paper is organized as follows. Firstly, the stochastic SR framework developed in Ref. 2 is briefly introduced in Section 2. Then a Grid-based MCMC SR framework is proposed in Section 3. Experimental results are presented in Section 4. Finally, Section 5 concludes this paper.

2. Stochastic Super-Resolution Imaging

2.1. *The Mathematical Framework of the SR Problem*

Given an original image, which is considered as the high-resolution ground truth, it is warped, blurred, downsampled and added with a zero-mean white Gaussian noise for simulating the observed low-resolution images. The above operations can be mathematically expressed as

$$\mathbf{y}^{(k)} = \mathbf{H}^{(k)}\mathbf{X} + \mathbf{V}^{(k)}, \tag{1}$$

where $\mathbf{y}^{(k)}$ and $\mathbf{X}$ represent the k-th low-resolution image and the high-resolution image, respectively. The matrix $\mathbf{H}^{(k)}$ represents the above-mentioned warping, convolving and downsampling processes, and the vector $\mathbf{V}^{(k)}$ represents the additive noise.

2.2. *Bayesian Inference*

The posterior distribution of the high-resolution image given the low-resolution observations can be rewritten by the Bayes rule as

$$p\left(\mathbf{X}|\mathbf{Y}\right) = \frac{p\left(\mathbf{X}, \mathbf{Y}\right)}{p\left(\mathbf{Y}\right)} \propto p\left(\mathbf{X}, \mathbf{Y}\right) = p\left(\mathbf{Y}|\mathbf{X}\right) p\left(\mathbf{X}\right). \tag{2}$$

Then, assume that the low-resolution images are obtained independently from the high-resolution image. According to (1), $p(\mathbf{Y}|\mathbf{X})$ is expressed as

$$p\left(\mathbf{Y}|\mathbf{X}\right) = \prod_{k=1}^{\rho} p\left(\mathbf{y}^{(k)}|\mathbf{X}\right) \propto \exp\left(-\frac{1}{2\sigma_v^2} \sum_{k=1}^{\rho} \left\|\mathbf{y}^{(k)} - \mathbf{H}^{(k)}\mathbf{X}\right\|^2\right). \tag{3}$$

Next, the prior image model with the expectation that the edge could be enhanced at the edge pixel positions while the image is locally smooth is

$$p(\mathbf{X}) \propto \exp\left\{-\frac{1}{2}\left(\lambda(\mathbf{E} \cdot \mathbf{X})^T \mathbf{C}(\mathbf{E} \cdot \mathbf{X}) + \beta(\mathbf{E} \cdot \mathbf{X})^T \mathbf{G}(\mathbf{E} \cdot \mathbf{X})\right)\right\}, \tag{4}$$

where the entries of $\mathbf{C}$ are given by $C_{i,j} = \gamma$, if $i = j$; $C_{i,j} = -1$, if i and j both fall in the γ-neighbourhood; otherwise, $C_{i,j} = 0$. Furthermore, $\mathbf{E}$ is the edge map of $\mathbf{X}$ with the entries being 1 at the edge pixel positions and 0 at the rest positions, the entries of $\mathbf{G}$ are given by $G_{i,j} = 1 + \frac{1}{\beta}$, if $i = j$; $C_{i,j} = -\frac{1}{\gamma}$, if i and j both fall in the γ-neighbourhood; otherwise, $G_{i,j} = 0$. Finally, substituting (3) and (4) into (2), $p\left(\mathbf{X}|\mathbf{Y}\right)$ can be obtained as

$$\begin{aligned} p(\mathbf{X}|\mathbf{Y}) \propto \exp\bigg\{ &-\frac{1}{2\sigma_v^2} \sum_{k=1}^{\rho} \left\|\mathbf{y}^{(k)} - \mathbf{H}^{(k)}\mathbf{X}\right\|^2 \\ &-\frac{1}{2}\left(\lambda(\mathbf{E} \cdot \mathbf{X})^T \mathbf{C}(\mathbf{E} \cdot \mathbf{X}) + \beta(\mathbf{E} \cdot \mathbf{X})^T \mathbf{G}(\mathbf{E} \cdot \mathbf{X})\right)\bigg\}. \end{aligned} \tag{5}$$

The goal of the MCMC SR approach is to estimate the high-resolution image by generating N image samples $\mathbf{X}^{(1)}, \ldots, \mathbf{X}^{(N)}$ from $p(\mathbf{X}|\mathbf{Y})$. Furthermore, the initially-generated T samples are considered unreliable and thus should be discarded. Finally, the high-resolution image is obtained by computing the mean of the follow-up generated $(N - T)$ samples; that is [2]

$$\hat{\mathbf{X}} = \frac{1}{N - T} \sum_{i=T+1}^{N} \mathbf{X}^{(i)}, \tag{6}$$

where the parameter T was derived in Ref. 2.

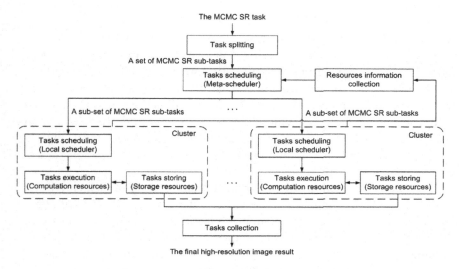

Figure 2.   An overview of the proposed Grid-based MCMC SR framework.

3. Grid Computing for Stochastic Super-resolution Imaging

Summarizing the previous Section, the MCMC SR approach developed in [2] requires fairly huge computational resources, due to the following two reasons: i) it needs to generate a fairly huge number of image samples for estimating the unknown high-resolution image; ii) it needs exhaustive search for obtaining the optimal model parameter value λ and β, for they intimately controls the degree of the regularity and the quality of the reconstructed high-resolution image.

To tackle the above computation challenge, the idea is to split the complicated MCMC SR task into a set of small and independent sub-tasks for parallel processing in the Grid computing environment [5], as demonstrated in Figure 2. Firstly, a number of independent and relatively small sub-tasks are assigned by the meta-scheduler to the available clusters in the Gird computing environment. Then, the local scheduler is exploited to further dispatch the sub-sets of MCMC SR sub-tasks across different available compute nodes, for executing these sub-tasks and exploiting the storage resources for storing the data and intermediate results. Finally, their results are assembled to select the best one (in terms of the PSNR) as the final result of the entire MCMC SR task.

4. Experimental Results

In our simulation, the low-resolution images are independently generated from the original image by applying shift and rotation on the test image, followed by the convoluting with a Gaussian low-pass filter with a size of 4×4 and a standard derivation of 2. Lastly, the processed image is down-sampled in both the horizontal and the vertical directions, and then added with a zero-mean Gaussian white noise with a standard derivation of 5. In our simulation, the permissible value range of λ and β are experimentally selected to be $[1, 50]$, and only integer values are used. The parameter ϵ is set to be 10, γ is set to be 4, and $N = 10 \times T$.

The proposed Grid-based MCMC SR framework is implemented and tested on the Grid computing environment offered by *National Grid Office* (NGO), Singapore. The grid computing facilities we used is composed of six compute nodes, each of which comprises two Intel Xeon 2.4G Hz CPUs running *Sun Grid Engine* (SGE) 5.3 as the local scheduler for each cluster.

The first experiment is to exploit the performance of the proposed Grid-based edge-adaptive MCMC SR approach and compare it with that of the *bi-cubic interpolation* approach. Figure 3 presents the results obtained from the test image *Airplane*. As seen from Figure 3, the proposed method yields superior performance to that of the bi-cubic interpolation approach.

Furthermore, the second experiment is conducted to compare the computational time of the proposed Grid-based MCMC SR approach with that of the single-PC-based MCMC SR approach developed in Ref. 2. The later approach is implemented on a single PC with a Pentium 2.4 GHz CPU and a 512 MB RAM. With the benefit from Grid computing, the computational time of the MCMC SR approach has been effectively reduced by 85.10%.

5. Conclusions

In this paper, Grid computing has been successfully exploited to overcome the computation challenge of the MCMC SR approach developed in Ref. 2, by splitting the computationally-intensive SR task into a set of independent and small sub-tasks dispatched for parallel processing. Extensive experimental results verify that Grid computing can effectively accelerate the execution time of the stochastic SR approach.

Acknowledgement

The authors would like to express their gratitude to National Grid Office (NGO), Singapore, for offering the Grid computing facilities.

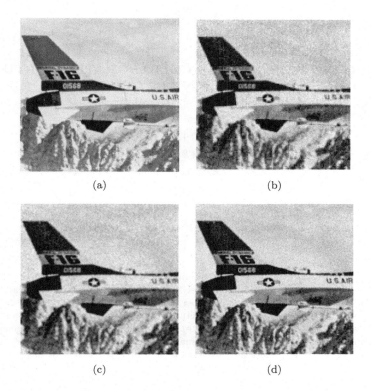

(a)　　　　　　　　　　　　(b)

(c)　　　　　　　　　　　　(d)

Figure 3. Various results of *Airplane* image (2×2 enlargement): (a) the original image; (b) synthesized low-resolution image (with pixel duplication for presentation); (c) the bi-cubic interpolation approach (PSNR = 25.69 dB); and (d) the proposed Grid-based edge-adaptive MCMC SR approach (PSNR = 29.53 dB).

References

1. M. G. Kang and S. Chaudhuri, *IEEE Signal Processing Mag.* **20**, 19(May 2003).
2. J. Tian and K.-K. Ma, A MCMC approach for Bayesian super-resolution image reconstruction, in *Proc. IEEE Int. Conf. on Image Processing*, Sept. 2005.
3. M. Parashar and C. Lee, *Special Issue on Grid Computing, Proceedings of the IEEE* **93**(Mar. 2003).
4. S. Hastings, T. Kurc, S. Langella, U. Catalyurek, T. Pan and J. Saltz, Image processing for the Grid: A toolkit for building Grid-enabled image processing applications, in *Proc. IEEE Symp. on Cluster Computing and the Grid*, May 2003.
5. J. Tian and K.-K. Ma, Super-resolution imaging using Grid computing, in *Proc. IEEE Symp. on Cluster Computing and the Grid*, May 2007.

SUPPORTING LARGE-SCALE COLLABORATIVE VIRTUAL ENVIRONMENT IN GRID*

LIANG ZHANG, QINGPING LIN, HOON KANG NEO,
GUANGBIN HUANG, ROBERT GAY and GUORUI FENG

Information Communication Institute of Singapore
School of Electrical and Electronic Engineering
Nanyang Technological University
50 Nanyang Avenue, Singapore 639798
E-mail: zhangliang@ntu.edu.sg, iqplin@ntu.edu.sg

The existing Collaborative Virtual Environment (CVE) systems have limited scalability due to the constraints in computer processing power and network bandwidth of participating hosts. In this paper, we propose a grid-based large-scale collaborative virtual environment architecture to scale across multiple geographically dispersed resources. The architecture consists of distributed mobile agents working cooperatively in supporting and managing the collaborative virtual environments. The mobile agents are autonomous and have the ability of migrating among hosts to maximize resource utilizations. Grid technologies allow the mobile agents to execute and communicate securely in multiple administrative domains. Grid-based scheduling components and polices can be integrated to provide intelligent resource optimizations. The result will be a more scalable architecture for supporting large-scale collaborative virtual environment.

1. Introduction

Collaborative Virtual Environment(CVE) technology is used in numerous application domains for users to experience shared sense of space and presence. It provides additional dimensions of communications,[1] offering users the ability to interact with each other in a common context. However, due to the heterogeneous nature of the Internet, system scalability in delivering virtual world database and maintaining consistent world states across all participants in a CVE become more challenging. This is particularly true if a CVE may have potentially a very large number of users at a time, whose real-time interactions can easily overload a fast network. As computing

---

*This work is supported by SERC Grant 052 015 0024 of A*STAR, Singapore.

resources are limited, obvious problems will arise once the number of users in a CVE rises beyond a certain limit. One may expect a CVE to produce undesirable effects such as choppy rendering, loss of interactivity, and alike, due to lack of processing power to handle the ever-increasing load. If such a case occurs, the collaboration will be lost. Although widely researched, scalability has remained as one of the main challenges in LCVE systems.

Over the years, various approaches and techniques have been researched and developed. They can be broadly grouped into two classes: interest management and effective communication architecture. In interest management, the spatial division of virtual space and introduction of entity auras are among some of the popular methods. They are aimed at reducing the message exchanges without harming the shared context and interactive performance.[3] On the other hand, the effective communication architecture approach adopts different network topologies and protocols in dealing with scalability issues. Peer-to-peer, federated peer-to-peer,[4] client-server, and multicasting[5] are among some of the popular methods.

The work in Ref. 2 has highlighted a need for flexible approach to the scalability problem. It proposed a Mobile Agent based CVE (MACVE). Mobile agent paradigm has been identified as the possible solution. It is based on the idea of mobile codes or processes that can migrate from one host to another, continuing its executions after the migrations.[8] Using a mobile agent oriented approach, the LCVE can be constructed using mobile agents. These agents are assigned with different and overlapping tasks like user interactions, system maintenances, and resource managements, etc. They work cooperatively to maintain the virtual worlds and the system. While mobile agent systems are flexible and agile, the Grid will be able to provide additional reliability and scalability needed.[6] In this paper, grid tools and concepts have been introduced into the MACVE architecture.

2. Grid-Based MACVE Architecture

The Grid-based MACVE is an extension of our existing system-MACVE.[2] The mobile agents will be able to migrate among resources that are located in different administrative domains. The agents' tasks includes high level LCVE supporting roles like maintaining world states consistencies, user interactions, scenes updating, and graphics rendering etc. Moreover, the agents' tasks also include low level system resource management roles like agent and computing resource discovery, scheduling, and monitoring, etc. More details of the MACVE architecture can be found in Ref. 2.

Grid-based MACVE is designed to have the capability of scaling and adapting in a Grid environment. Scalability, autonomy and security are among the ultimatums of its design and architecture. It is envisioned as a distributed infrastructure with its components(agents) spreading across multiple virtual organizations (VO).[7] The system will have the ability of growing to meet the demand imposed by the LCVE it is supporting. In this paper, we will discuss three main areas of the Grid-based MACVE architecture: Grid-based mobile agent environment, Resource discovery and monitoring, Resource scheduling and load balancing.

2.1. Grid-Based Mobile Agent Environment

The Mobile Agent Environments (MAEs), are essentially agent containers residing in all the participating nodes.They are holistic environments where the mobile agent can execute securely in. The MAEs control the agent execution and migration, help agents to communicate with each other, and monitor the resource information about the node and the local agents.

In the Grid-based MACVE, MAEs can exist in the forms of WSRF Grid services for secure communication. The MAEs communicate with each other by invoking the counterpart's services. There are three main services identified here: Agent Management Service, Agent Messaging Service and MAE Monitoring Service.

2.1.1. Agent Management Service

Agent Management Service is one of the major component of the MAE, which provides the agent execution and migration management. The mobile agent's execution, migration, synchronization and hand-over at the remote MAEs in different administrative domains can be enabled by invoking the different operations in Agent Management Service.

The agent migration process in MAE is sender-initiated, invoked by the agent itself. In order to migrate to another MAE, the mobile agent must explicitly invoke a move(destination) primitive under its own control. This, in a way, enables user to design and implement mobile agents with high level of autonomy. The agent migration process include three steps: agent code transferring, agent state synchronization, agent control handover, which are the combination of the mutual service calls at sender's and receiver's MAE. As the agent code may be big in size, GridFTP and RFT will be incorporate in Agent Management Service in our future works.

2.1.2. *Agent Messaging Service*

In the Grid-based MACVE environment, communication is a critical part of the system. The mobile agents need an efficient, reliable and secured communication infrastructure. WSRF and GSI in GT 4 provide a uniform and reliable way for data communication. Agent Messaging Service is designed as a WSRF-compliant component to help the local agents send and receive messages. The Agent Messaging Service forwards the local agent messages to the remote agents by invoking the Agent Messaging Service of the remote MAE. After receiving the messages, the remote Agent Messaging Service will dispatch the messages to the corresponding agents.

To reduce the complexity, the remote agent location is transparent to the local agent. The Agent Messaging Service resolute the remote agent location by invoking the Agent Addressing Services(discussed in Section 2.2) with the remote agent ID.

2.1.3. *MAE Monitoring Service*

To support a scalable and reliable distributed resource discovery mechanism in MACVE, each MAE provides a monitoring service to capture the resource information about the host and the local agents, which include host resource and workload information, agent performance information and agent addressing information. As a information provider, MAE Monitoring Service publishes the collected information to different index services via WS-ResourceProperty and WS-Notification mechanisms.

2.2. *Resource Discovery and Monitoring*

One of the fundamental and core requirements of the Grid-based MACVE is resource discovery and monitoring. Resource discovery, in MACVE's context, means the detection of the nodes with enough resource to host agents, and the resolution of agent current network location. In correspondence with the information provided by MAE Monitor Services, MACVE provides three types of aggregator services: host performance index service, agent performance index service and agent addressing index service.

Each VO may maintain one or more of index services. These index services provide distributed aggregated information for proper execution of agents and services in MACVE. For examples, Group Manager Agent[2] subscribes to the host performance index service and agent performance index service in its VO to get the information for agent scheduling. Agent

Addressing Service query agent addressing index services to find out the current agent address.

2.3. *MACVE Scheduling and Load Balancing*

Scheduling of applications has always been one of the main challenges in Grid Computing. The problem of scheduling and load balancing in the MACVE can be viewed as trying to assign or arrange n number of mobile agents with different workloads, to m number of hosts with different capacities. In MACVE, the agent scheduling and load balancing is based on MDS services. Agent dependencies information can be published as agent meta data so that the Group Manage Agent (the scheduler) can have more types of information to optimize the decision.

On the other hand, the measurement of the workload of the individual mobile agents will be a difficult task to perform. The historical data will be used in the Group Manager Agent to predict the future agents' workloads by self-learning algorithms.

3. Implementation and Evaluation

We have developed a prototype grid-based LCVE system using GT4 and Cortona VRML Client. Currently, there are 10 grid nodes in our Infor-Comm Research Lab to host the LCVE system. The users using web browser with Cortona VRML client as plug-in can join the LCVE. In the virtual environment, there are multiple types of virtual entities. Users can walk in it, add/delete virtual entities, collaboratively interact with the virtual entities, and communicate with each other by text message chat. As shown in Figure 1, we use 50 RobotGroup Agents running at different machines to simulate 1000 concurrent users and 5000 virtual entities.

4. Conclusions

In this paper, we have proposed a grid-based LCVE architecture that has the capability of scaling reliably across multiple geographically dispersed resources. This architecture is designed to be flexible, autonomous and scalable. We have implemented and tested the proposed approach in our prototype system: grid-based MACVE. We will further evaluate the performance of our proposed approach using large-scale CVE system with tens of thousands of virtual entities. Our future work will also include development of intelligent real-time self-learning algorithms for LCVE task scheduling, load balancing and user interaction message routing in grid based MACVE.

Figure 1. Screenshot of a user host interacts with grid-based LCVE.

References

1. S. Singhal and M. Zyda, *Networked virtual environments: design and implementation.* New York, NY, USA: ACM Press/Addison-Wesley Publishing Co., 1999.
2. L. Zhang and Q. Lin, "Macve: A mobile agent based framework for large-scale collaborative virtual environments," *accepted by Presence: Teleoper. Virtual Environ.*, 2006.
3. D. Lee, M. Lim, and S. Han, "Atlas - a scalable network framework for distributed virtual environments," *Proceedings of the 4th International Conference on Collaborative Virtual Environments*, pp. 47 – 54, 2002.
4. S. Rooney, D. Bauer, and R. Deydier, "A federated peer-to-peer network game architecture," *IEEE Communications Magazine*, vol. 42, no. 5, pp. 114 – 22, 2004.
5. C. Joslin, T. Di Giacomo, and N. Magnenat-Thalmann, "Collaborative virtual environments: From birth to standardization," *IEEE Communications Magazine*, vol. 42, no. 4, pp. 28 – 33, 2004.
6. I. Foster, N. R. Jennings, and C. Kesselman, "Brain meets brawn: Why grid and agents need each other," *Proceedings of the Third International Joint Conference on Autonomous Agents and Multiagent Systems, AAMAS 2004*, vol. 1, pp. 8 – 15, 2004.
7. I. Foster, C. Kesselman, J. Nick, and S. Tuecke, "The physiology of the grid: An open grid services architecture for distributed systems integration," *Open Grid Service Infrastructure WG, Global Grid Forum*, 2002.
8. W. R. Cockayne and M. Zyda, *Mobile agents.* Manning Pubns Co, 1997.

DESIGNING AN EXPERIMENTAL GAMING PLATFORM FOR TRADING GRID RESOURCES

DANNY OH, CHENG SHIH-FEN and MA DAN

School of Information Systems
Singapore Management University

RAVI BAPNA

Centre for Information Technology and the Networked Economy
Indian School of Business

This paper describes our current work in designing an experimental gaming platform for simulating the trading of grid resources. The open platform allows researchers in grid economics to experiment with different market structures and pricing models. We would be using a design science approach in the implementation. Key design considerations and an overview of the functional design of the platform are presented and discussed.

1. Introduction

Utility computing is a recent and exciting development in IT outsourcing whereby IT resources are provided as needed and the customer pays only for actual use. Companies who wish to provide shared computing facilities to customers often face the challenge on how to price their services. For example, Sun, IBM and HP have all adopted the fixed price model for various practical reasons. However, the fixed price model may not lead to an economically-efficient resource allocation, especially when market demand is high and volatile. The question then arises as to what economic market mechanisms are suitable for facilitating price discovery and economic valuation based resource allocation for shared computing services. Currently, little market data is available to test the efficacy of current approaches. Yet, such data are critical to build and test theories of consumer behavior and choice in the utility computing context. In addition, the experimental data provide a data source in situations where relevant field data cannot be obtained. This motivates us to develop an experimental platform for understanding the dynamics of trading of computing resources.

2. Motivation

To do research in grid economics, it is essential for researchers to have a platform which allows them to design and test various market models and pricing strategies. To the best of our knowledge, there is no such publicly available simulation system yet. In this work, we use the design science approach [5] to conceptualize a novel IT artifact that permits real human players and automated agents to trade in computing resources to accomplish jobs for which they have monetary values, as well as to sell unused computing capacity on their networked machines.

3. Design Science Approach

As per Hevner *et al.* (2004), the first step in pursuing the design science approach is to design an IT artifact. In that spirit, the availability of an open-sourced market simulation system will allow researchers to conduct experiments on various pricing mechanisms such as different types of auction and negotiation models, posted price model, and different tariff structures of pricing models. These pricing and allocation mechanisms will be evaluated in the context of an experimental trading environment that is designed using the principles of induced value theory [12].

4. Research Contributions

The key research question of this work is to evaluate various market models and pricing strategies for the trading of grid resources so as to make recommendations for suitable ones. Additionally, we are also interested to find out how uniform and discriminatory pricing schemes compare viz efficiency and fairness given rationally bounded agents? Finally, we are keen to determine if it is feasible to introduce spot and future prices for CPU and storage commodities.

5. Market Game Simulation Platform

Instead of developing a full fledged market simulation system from scratch, we will take advantage of existing systems which have already been developed for the running of market games. Examples of such systems include AB3D [6], AuctionBot [8], e-Game [7], eMediator [11] and Meet2Trade [2]. To the best of our knowledge, the only openly available system is AB3D. Therefore, in this project, we will use AB3D as the software foundation for our development.

For all these scenarios, there are two major components: 1) agents that represent individual decision makers, and 2) market mechanisms that allow exchange of resources. Due to the decentralized nature of the problem, most agent-specific information, including preferences over tasks, capabilities in performing tasks and resource holdings, are endowed to each agent. Moreover, probability distributions are usually used in describing much of this information to account for uncertainties involved in the problem. This probabilistic representation of the problem makes it very difficult to analytically evaluate the performances of combinations of strategies.

To estimate the performances of combinations of strategies, we can define a market game as a collection of agents and market mechanisms, and execute Monte Carlo simulations, in which each agent's related information is generated according to the governing distribution. The AB3D platform is developed to support massive simulation efforts. In the following paragraphs, we provide more details on the various components of the platform. The interactions of the above components are illustrated in Figure 1.

- **Scripting auction engine**. AB3D supports a wide range of market mechanisms, specified in a high-level rule-based auction scripting language. The scripting language exposes parameters characterizing the space of bidding, information revelation, and allocation policies [9]. With proper programming constructs, flow control can also be easily achieved.

- **Market game engine**. To generate a market game probabilistically, we need to provide both common information and agent-specific information, as described as follows:

  o *Common information*: this refers to important information agents should know even before the game is actually executed. Most common information is related to the structure of the game, including (but not limited to): i) length of the game, ii) number of agents in the game, and their respective roles, if any (e.g., buyer, seller), and iii) number and type of auctions used in the game.

  o *Agent-specific information*: in a typical decentralized resource allocation problem, each agent is endowed with information that is only accessible to itself. This information may include task properties (e.g., the value for fulfilling the task, the deadline of the task, and the resource requirement of the task), and initial resource endowment. To support probabilistic game generation, a set of programming constructs, called game description language (GDL) is developed to support basic variable declarations, looping, and random variable generations. A detailed description on GDL is available in Ref. 10.

- **Agent interface**. The game system implements a communication interface through which bids, queries, and any other game interactions are transmitted.
- **Scorer**. The scorer evaluates the performance of each agent at the end of each game. Scoring typically entails the assembly of transactions to determine final holdings, and for each agent, an allocation of resources to activities maximizing its own objective function. For each agent and the strategy it represents, this score indicates how well it performs in this particular strategy combination for some realization of the agent preferences.
- **Market control room**. An important element of the design science approach is to build in an iterative methodology that searches for gaps between the design objectives and the observed metrics. To achieve this, a market control room will be created which is under the control of the researcher. It takes as input the performance metrics, such as efficiency measures and profits, from the monitoring of the market and sets a variety of system level parameters that are in constant need of fine tuning and exploration.
- **WS-Agreement Generator**. The outcome of the games (i.e. resources to be allocated per agent) will be composed as WS-Agreements. WS-Agreement is a XML based language and protocol designed for advertising the capabilities of resource providers and creating service agreements, and for monitoring agreement compliance at runtime. It is the proposed standard for the Grid Resource Allocation Agreement Protocol [4].

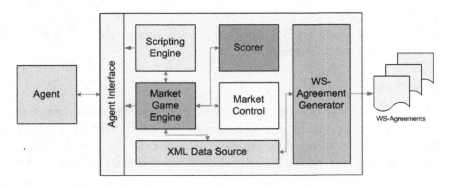

Figure 1: General market gaming platform, depicted at functional level.

With this general market gaming platform, we can execute large number of simulations in order to accurately estimate the payoff for each agent strategy in a strategy combination. Note that since it is possible that multiple copies of the same strategy may appear in a strategy combination, when estimating the payoff associated with some strategy, we compute the average payoff for all agents using this strategy, and let the average payoff be the estimated payoff of this strategy.

6. Market and Pricing Models

We plan to use the market gaming platform to experiment with different market models. Existing literature focuses more on market-based models [1,3]. Therefore, in the initial phase, we plan to support the commodity market model and auction model first. Other models such as bargaining model and tendering model will be supported in subsequent phases.

We also plan to experiment with different pricing models. We will take the fixed pricing model as benchmark, and study and compare it with other pricing models. We are interested in examining how vendor profit, consumer surplus, as well as social welfare will change under different pricing models. As a result, we are able to identify the optimal resource allocation strategy.

In the initial phase, we will focus on different variations of the auction-based pricing. In particular, we are very interested to model the market as a multi-attribute combinatorial exchange since it allows multiple buyers and sellers to simultaneously submit bids on heterogeneous services. Support for other models such as multi-part tariffs will be available in subsequent phases.

Since different businesses have different requirements, goals, policies and strategies, we expect a grid market to support a variety of market models. It is important to understand how each of these models affects allocation fairness, system efficiency and performance.

7. Conclusion

In this paper, we describe our current work in developing an experimental gaming platform for trading of grid resources. We also describe key design considerations such as the different ways of commoditizing grid resources, market structures and pricing models which have significant impacts in the design of the platform. Moving forward, we would be concentrating on developing the gaming platform and designing games for real players and automated agents involving the trading of grid resources. We hope to use the platform to gather data that will help us answer our research questions and to further understand the entire Grid economy concept.

References

1. Bapna, R., Sanjukta Das, Robert Garfinkel, and Jan Staellert, Market Design for Grid Computing, forthcoming in the *INFORMS Journal on Computing*.
2. D. Neumann, C. Holtmann, H. Weltzien, C. Lattemann, and Ch. Weinhardt. Towards a generic e-market design. In *Towards the Knowledge Society: e-Commerce, e-Business and e-Government*. Kluwer Academic Publishers, 2002.
3. Danny Oh, Steven Miller, and Hu Nan, Experimental and Empirical Perspectives on Grid Resource Allocation for the Singapore Market, In *Proceedings of the 3rd International Workshop on Grid Economics and Business Models*, May 2006, pp. 13-23.
4. GRAAP-WG, G. G. F., 2006. Grid resource allocation agreement protocol. https://forge.gridforum.org/projects/graap-wg.
5. Hevner, A., March, S. T., Park, J., and John, S. Design Science Research in Information Systems, *MIS Quarterly* (28:1) March 2004, pp. 75-105.
6. Kevin M. Lochner and Michael P. Wellman. Rule-based specification of auction mechanisms. In *Third International Joint Conference on Autonomous Agents and Multi-Agent Systems*, pages 818–825, 2004.
7. Maria Fasli and Michael Michalakopoulos. e-Game: A generic auction platform supporting customizable market games. In *IEEE/WIC/ACM International Conference on Intelligent Agent Technology* (IAT'04), pages 190–196, 2004.
8. Peter R. Wurman, Michael P. Wellman, and William E. Walsh. The Michigan Internet AuctionBot: A configurable auction server for human and software agents. In *Second International Conference on Autonomous Agents*, pages 301–308, Minneapolis, 1998.
9. Peter R. Wurman, Michael P. Wellman, and William E. Walsh. A parameterization of the auction design space, *Games and Economic Behavior*, 35:304–338, 2001.
10. Shih-Fen Cheng. Game-Theoretic Approaches for Complex Systems Optimization. PhD thesis, University of Michigan, 2006.
11. Tuomas Sandholm. eMediator: A next generation electronic commerce server. *Computational Intelligence: Special issue on Agent Technology for Electronic Commerce*, 18(4):656–676, 2004.
12. V. Smith. Experimental Economics: Induced Value Theory. *American Economic Review*, 66 (2), 1976. 274–279, May.